# Giving Voice to Children's Artistry

# Giving Voice to Children's Artistry

## A GUIDE FOR MUSIC TEACHERS AND CHORAL CONDUCTORS

**Mary Ellen Pinzino**

OXFORD
UNIVERSITY PRESS

# OXFORD
UNIVERSITY PRESS

Oxford University Press is a department of the University of Oxford. It furthers
the University's objective of excellence in research, scholarship, and education
by publishing worldwide. Oxford is a registered trade mark of Oxford University
Press in the UK and certain other countries.

Published in the United States of America by Oxford University Press
198 Madison Avenue, New York, NY 10016, United States of America.

© Oxford University Press 2022

Library of Congress Control Number: 2021033973
ISBN 978–0–19–760653–7 (pbk.)
ISBN 978–0–19–760652–0 (hbk.)

DOI: 10.1093/oso/9780197606520.001.0001

1 3 5 7 9 8 6 4 2

Paperback printed by Marquis, Canada
Hardback printed by Bridgeport National Bindery, Inc., United States of America

**Praise for** *Giving Voice to Children's Artistry*

This uniquely refreshing book offers meaningful perspectives into not just music teaching but something much more significant—cultivating children's artistry. Mary Ellen Pinzino's thoughtful insights and approaches, particularly to repertoire and teaching strategies, are certainly a major contribution to our profession! Wish this book had been available before I retired—it would have been a required text in both my undergraduate and graduate courses! In particular, Pinzino's "Song Architecture" is a unique and thoughtful approach to repertoire.

—Joanne Rutkowski, Professor Emeritus of Music Education, The Pennsylvania State University

I highly recommend this book for use in the music classroom, children's chorus, and training future music educators. The text is well laid out to enable sequential teaching and learning, and is compatible with the approaches of Orff, Kodaly, Dalcroze, and Gordon. There are many creative examples of teaching unusual rhythms and modal melodies that enhance musicianship of all ages, challenging students and teachers alike. The thoughtful texts and lovely melodies offer rich music learning resources and opportunities for all!

—Patricia Wurst Cichy, Assistant Professor of Music Education (retired), Providence College

Perhaps the most salient aspect of this beautifully written book is the unwavering respect Mary Ellen Pinzino shows for the musical artistry of every child. The music educator who takes to heart the principles of learning embedded within this book will be joyfully rewarded. They will discover that the adult impulse to "think in words" can be safely set aside as the musical artistry of each child is allowed to emerge. In so doing, the teacher may uncover aspects of their own inherent musicality. To me, this book was reminiscent of the profound respect for the child-as-musician evident in the work of Shinichi Suzuki and Émile Jaques-Dalcroze. The joy and wonder of music learning resonates on every page. The essential need to nurture the child's capacity to "think in music" resonates in every chapter. An exquisite gem.

—Roseanne Rosenthal, President, VanderCook College of Music

Approaching music teaching and learning through the portal of artistry is a desperately needed approach in teaching children. Using proven principles of Music Learning developed by Edwin Gordon that truly integrates music skill and long-term musical growth makes this a landmark publication. The realization that artistry begins and is fostered within the spirit of a child is, perhaps, the only place from which music can have a voice of honesty. In this book artistic spirit and the psychology of music learning become true partners.

—James Jordan, Professor, Westminster Choir College; Co-Director, The Choral Institute at Oxford

Mary Ellen Pinzino has captured the essence of children's inherent musical artistry, celebrating its wonder and splendor. She guides and empowers readers to trust, nurture, and revel in the exquisite beauty of children's musicality as they inspire children's artistic spirits to flourish.

—Suzanne L. Burton, Associate Dean for the Arts, University of Delaware

Packed with common sense suggestions for developing musical artistry, Mary Ellen Pinzino effectively engages the reader's thinking and musical minds. Readers will be inspired to reflect on their instructional practices and engage personally with the musical exercises carefully sequenced throughout this book.

—Alden H. Snell II, Associate Professor of Music Teaching and Learning, Eastman School of Music

My journey through Mary Ellen Pinzino's book has been invaluable and inspiring! Guided by her knowledgeable and encouraging voice, I have discovered the joy of unleashing children's artistry in both my general music classrooms and my choral rehearsals. Her songs are unique and delightful gems that evoke artistry and enthusiasm from teacher and students alike. Her compiled revelations gained through decades of teaching and conducting are absolute gold!

—Renee Vande Wege, Music Teacher and Choral Director, Rockford Michigan Public Schools

Mary Ellen Pinzino offers a proven and pragmatic approach for all music teachers to help surface and deepen children's musical minds. At its core, this is a book about an essential but often ignored pre-requisite for the artistry of leadership.

—Harry L. Davis, Distinguished Service Professor, Harry L. Davis Center for Leadership, University of Chicago

Mary Ellen Pinzino has authored an excellent guide for the development of "children's artistry." This book is a welcome resource for music teachers and those aspiring to engage students in artistry through experience.

—G. David Peters, Professor (retired), Music and Arts Technology, Indiana University—IUPUI

Pheasant," Figure 6.1 "Grasshopper," Figure 6.2 "Night," Figure 6.3 "A Pair of Butterflies," Figure 6.4 "A Lantern Dance," Figure 6.5 "Elephant," Figure 6.6 "Butterfly Dreams," Figure 6.7 "Dreams of Flowers," Figure 6.8 "Green Leaves in the Sunlight," Figure 6.9 "Dreams," Figure 6.10 "Autumn Thought," Figure 7.1 "A Merry Sparrow," Figure 7.2 "Turtle," Figure 7.3 "Lie A-Bed," Figure 7.4 "Parakeet," Figure 7.5 "Butterfly," Figure 7.6 "Dancing Girl," Figure 7.7 "Two Children," Figure 7.8 "Yak," Figure 7.9 "Autumn Dusk," Figure 7.10 "Giraffe," Figure 7.11 "Seahorse," Figure 7.12 "Dolphin," Figure 7.13 "April Rain Song," Figure 7.14 "Sea Anemone," Figure 7.15 "Fairies," Figure 7.16 "Snow Is Falling," Figure 7.17 "The Falling Star," Figure 7.18 "The Bow that Bridges Heaven." Songs and chants from the Come Children Sing Institute SONG LIBRARY, composed by Mary Ellen Pinzino, Copyright © 1997 Mary Ellen Pinzino. Used with permission.

# CONTENTS

# Introduction

My deepest desire is for children everywhere to experience the wonder of their own artistry.

I invite you to join me in unveiling children's artistry and enabling its brilliance. Giving voice to children's artistry can transform every music class and children's chorus into a community of artists making exciting music.

Children's artistry can be elusive. We might know it when we see it, but do we know it when we don't see it? Do we notice when it is not present in our music classes or rehearsals? Children's artistry is inherent in every child. It is up to us as music teachers to give it voice and bring it to the forefront of every music class and children's chorus, where it belongs.

This book makes the intangibles of children's artistry more tangible. Part 1 presents characteristic behaviors of children's artistry, its progression of development, and necessary components for growth, identifying four dimensions of the process of giving voice to children's artistry. "Awakening Artistry" opens the gateway to artistry in every child. "Moving Artistry" addresses the power of movement in the embodiment of children's artistry. "Inspiring Artistry" examines song and its role in the development of children's artistry. "Eliciting Artistry" offers techniques that facilitate children's artistry. Musical examples and songs are included to demonstrate principles presented. Part 2 presents Etudes designed to support the teacher in the practice of giving voice to children's artistry, and to provide materials for implementation in the music classroom and children's chorus. "Etude 1-For Starters," grounds the teacher and the children in getting started. "Etude 2-For Movement," guides the use of movement to improve performance at every level. "Etude 3-For Songs," offers songs that give voice to children's artistry and guides the process of selecting songs for children at various levels of development. Content is intended for application with children from kindergarten through seventh grade, though it is also appropriate with older singers in the process of developing artistry.

Every age and stage offers unique insights into the development of artistry. I have been fortunate in this field to have taught all ages from birth through graduate students. Teaching high school choral music, elementary classroom music, early childhood music, children's choruses, and college methods courses primed me for starting the Come Children Sing Institute as a center for research and development in music learning. Creating a comprehensive early childhood music program and children's choral program in that context provided the unique experience of working with many of the same

*Giving Voice to Children's Artistry.* Mary Ellen Pinzino, Oxford University Press. © Oxford University Press 2022.
DOI: 10.1093/oso/9780197606520.003.0001

children for ten or eleven years. Nurturing the development of children's artistry from early childhood through advanced choral performance necessitated ongoing inquiry into its developmental progression and the composition of many songs and materials to meet the musical needs of children of all ages and stages.

Studying extensively with Edwin Gordon for over ten years impacted my teaching and classroom research at the Come Children Sing Institute. Throughout many years as student, friend, and colleague, I wrote copious letters to him about what I was witnessing at the Institute with all ages and stages in relation to his research on music learning, and I enjoyed many long weekends of discussion with him on music learning as a guest in his home. I was also influenced by singing for a year in a church choir under the inspiring direction of Doreen Rao. I was delighted as friend and colleague to also be able to observe her work in rehearsals and performances with her then Glen Ellyn Children's Chorus and with children's choral festivals that included my own ensembles. I engaged for many years in the children's choral movement she spearheaded.

Viewing teaching and learning through many years in the music classroom and choral rehearsal from the perspective of both the process of music learning and choral artistry, with each informing the other, became most significant in my teaching and composing. Children's artistry revealed itself in children of all ages and stages in both classroom and choral contexts. Children clearly demonstrated that we can draw artistry out of every child and draw every child into the choral art.

Presenting at numerous music education and choral conferences and training music teachers and choral conductors both live and online through many years helped me to analyze and better understand the process of developing children's artistry in relation to both music learning and the choral art. Serving as choral conductor at one of the Chicago City Colleges and at the University of Illinois at Chicago, after so many years with children, supported my views on the development of artistry. A three-year collaboration with the adept Michael Anderson at UIC expanded my perspective and broadened my view of the power of movement in the choral rehearsal.

The icing on the cake of a long career, especially after having had my own sons in my music classes and children's choruses throughout their childhood, has been teaching two young grandsons weekly in the privacy of my own home. This intimate, ongoing view of the process of giving voice to children's artistry from early childhood to teen years has kept the principles presented here alive during the writing of this book, with the joy of developing artistry in these young boys second only to being the grandmother of four.

Children's artistry is a stunningly beautiful dimension of children of all ages. We can uncover it in every music class and children's chorus, whatever the methodology or conducting style, as it resides in children rather than in methodology or rehearsal technique. It is up to us as music teachers to make it come alive and to bring together the wonder of children and the wonder of the art itself in making exciting music.

Giving voice to children's artistry is one of the greatest joys of teaching music. May this book serve to give voice to children's artistry in your music classroom and chorus—and in the field of music education.

**PART 1**

# Awakening Artistry

Children's artistry is a wonder to behold! It is the heart and soul of the child intertwined with the heart and soul of the music. It is the beauty of the child interacting with the beauty of the line. It is the life force of the child engaged with the life force of the music.

Children's artistry is a powerful wellspring in every child. It makes exciting music. It builds lines, creates phrases, expresses musical nuance, and revels in the intertwining of text, rhythm, and melody. Children's artistry resonates with the art itself—the art that drew each of us into this field.

Children's artistry is joyful. It is shy. It is vulnerable. Children are very protective of their artistry. They will often engage in music activities without risking its exposure. Children's artistry knows when a music activity does not merit its presence, and will show its face only in a context that excites musical sensitivity.

It is up to us as music teachers and choral conductors to provide the environment that awakens children's artistry and compels it to reveal itself, yet children's artistry is a topic that is not often addressed in music methods courses. An understanding of children's artistry and how to nurture it can serve every age, context, and methodology. Giving voice to children's artistry leads to greater musicality in every classroom and chorus. Giving voice to the development of children's artistry leads to expanding horizons in music education.

Two major advances in our field in the past fifty years shed light on children's artistry. Extensive research, spearheaded by Edwin Gordon, has led to greater understanding of the process of music learning, while the ever-expanding children's choral movement, spearheaded by Doreen Rao, has successfully translated the choral art and vocal technique to young voices.

The influence of these forces at the Come Children Sing Institute, in both early childhood music classes and children's choruses, was profound. Children from tots to teens grew by leaps and bounds. Every age and stage of development led to new insights that could be applied to others. Children who began as little children and returned every year for ten or eleven years offered the unique challenge of meeting children's ongoing musical needs from early childhood through advanced children's chorus. Extensive searching and "re-searching" in the classroom revealed how the process of music learning grows into artistry. Applying insights learned to all ages and stages as well as to college choruses unveiled the process of growing into choral artistry independent of age.

*Giving Voice to Children's Artistry.* Mary Ellen Pinzino, Oxford University Press. © Oxford University Press 2022.
DOI: 10.1093/oso/9780197606520.003.0002

You may recognize the influence of Edwin Gordon, Doreen Rao, and others, filtered through years of classroom research. Ideas presented here have evolved through many years with hundreds of children of all ages and stages in both classroom and choral contexts, and with college choruses. Developing children's artistry is an ongoing process that spans context, age, and methodology. It blurs the line between classroom music and children's chorus, as well as the line between early childhood music and classroom music. Giving voice to children's artistry is the goal that unites us as music teachers.

## Getting Started

The four chapters in Part 1 of this book work in tandem with each other. "Awakening Artistry," "Moving Artistry," "Inspiring Artistry," and "Eliciting Artistry" go hand-in-hand, with each dimension enhancing the other. Trying an occasional idea presented here is not going to turn your children into artists. Uncovering children's artistry takes time. It takes ongoing effort. It takes the determination to search and re-search in your own classroom or children's chorus to bring to life the untapped artistry in your own children, which can only make your children more musical and your teaching more fulfilling.

Some of the ideas presented here may align with your current practices or methodology, while others may seem foreign to you. You may find it necessary to stretch beyond your comfort zone to explore children's artistry. Perhaps you are not yet comfortable with movement in the classroom or choral rehearsal. Perhaps you are not yet comfortable with art songs with inexperienced singers, or you have worked primarily with developed singers. Perhaps you have taught only instrumental or early childhood music and are not yet comfortable engaging in the choral art. The Etudes in Part 2 of this book will help you to develop both competence and confidence in giving voice to children's artistry, and they provide materials for implementation in your music classroom or children's chorus.

Children will also help you to find your way, as children revel in their own artistry. Every age and stage offers insights that can guide you with others. Every class you teach offers a new perspective from which to witness the unfolding of children's artistry.

Your unique journey in this field, with all your strengths and weaknesses, provides a platform of solid gold from which to view the development of children's artistry. Any perceived lack you might feel in skill, training, or experience will lead you to insights that you may not otherwise have been able to discover. The area in which you might feel least competent provides an opening from which you can view emerging artistry in a way that colleagues you might feel to be more accomplished cannot. You just have to be willing to fully explore each of the various dimensions of developing artistry and how they work together, and give yourself the needed time to grow—*to become an artist*—in giving voice to children's artistry.

## Speaking the Language

Awakening artistry in the music classroom or children's chorus requires that we learn to speak the language of the musical mind. We most often speak the language of the thinking mind, assuming that our well-meaning words are reaching and teaching the musical mind. Words do not speak to the musical mind. Language actually gets in the way of the musical mind and interrupts its focus. The thinking mind processes words. The musical mind processes rhythm and melody. Words capture the imagination of the thinking mind. Rhythm, melody, and accompanying movement capture the imagination of the musical mind.

We have become so accustomed to speaking to the thinking mind in our music classrooms and rehearsals that we inadvertently shut out the musical mind. Our inviting instructions, thoughtful explanations, questions, charming stories, and imagery speak to the thinking mind. The more we address the thinking mind, the more the musical mind lies dormant.

It is the musical mind we must learn to address if we want to engage children's artistry. It is the musical mind that generates in-tune singing, rhythmic delivery, and the energy of the line in all its nuance. It is the musical mind that gives rise to children's artistry. We have to let go of our wordiness in the music classroom and choral rehearsal so that children's artistry can literally have its say.

Pure rhythm and pure melody are the mother tongue of the musical mind. They speak the language the musical mind understands. Unadorned rhythm and melody compel the musical mind without words, props, or imagery—accompanied only by movement.

We all know that we can capture the imagination of a group of children and hold it in the palm of our hand with a good story. Yet we fail to believe that we can do the same with the musical imagination. We seem to think that we have to prop up pure rhythm or melody with word narratives, games, or explanations. The "narrative" that holds the musical mind captive is not a story tied together with musical segments or a story wrapped in music, but rather, pure rhythm or melody.

Interrupting the musical narrative to instruct, explain, or talk to children is the aural equivalent of walking in front of a TV screen, interrupting viewing. Words break the spell created by the power of rhythm and melody. The musical narrative, without the interruption of words, transports the musical mind to the wonder of its own artistry.

Speaking the language of the thinking mind places the thinking mind at the forefront of our music classes and choral rehearsals and silences the musical mind. Speaking the language of the musical mind brings the musical mind to the forefront, moving the thinking mind to the background. Like the vase and face optical illusion, both the thinking mind and the musical mind are accessible, but the foreground and the background are entirely different depending on our focus. We have to be deliberate to keep our sights on the musical mind if we want to reach children's artistry.

The thinking mind is reticent to engage in musicality when it is at the forefront. It is self-conscious and judgmental, perhaps declaring this song or that music activity to be boring. It views music from the outside. The musical mind when dominant in the classroom or rehearsal views music from the inside, embracing songs and activities worthy of its artistry. It becomes so compelled by musicality that it loses all sense of self.

The child whose thinking mind is at the forefront in the music class is like the daydreaming child in an academic class. Both have to be brought back to "reality," with musicality being the reality in the music classroom. The more we engage the musical mind, the more present children become in our classes and rehearsals and the more musical our classrooms and ensembles become.

We, as a field of music education, have so relied on words to teach music—to address style, vocal technique, text, note values, instructions, expectations, and questions—that we have neglected children's artistry. We must bring the musical mind to the forefront, become fluent in its language, and unleash the power of the musical mind. Only then can we give voice to children's artistry.

## Making Sense

The musical mind has much to teach us about children's artistry. It becomes increasingly transparent as we learn to speak its mother tongue and bring it to the forefront of our teaching. It then communicates freely, revealing its capabilities, needs, and its differences from the thinking mind, informing our teaching at every level.

Children are wired for rhythm and melody, needing immersion and interaction in the language of the musical mind to develop that innate capacity, just as children are wired for language and require immersion and interaction in language to develop that innate capacity. The musical mind needs a "sound environment" within which it can "make sense" of rhythm and melody—a sense of rhythm and a sense of pitch. Understanding how the musical mind "makes sense" guides us in creating a "sound environment" in which we can awaken artistry in all children.

Individual beats or individual pitches do not "make sense" to the musical mind, as it attends to beats in relation to each other and pitches in relation to each other. The organization of beats gives rise to meter, with different meters defined by unique beat groupings. The organization of pitches gives rise to tonality, with different tonalities defined by the particular arrangement of pitches in relation to a resting tone. It is meter and tonality that stir the musical mind.

The thought of various meters and tonalities may conjure up long-forgotten theoretical definitions of meters and modes, and insecurities about having command of these "sound structures." Be assured that a willingness to explore will help to conquer self-doubts while leading you to discover something mighty powerful in the music classroom.

Meter and tonality enchant the musical imagination. They provide the gateway to children's artistry. They offer the language with which we can awaken the musical mind. They provide the raw material for the musical narratives that bring the musical mind to the forefront of our classrooms, without words, without props, without explanations, accompanied only by movement.

Meter and tonality have power over the musical mind that is hard to imagine with our thinking minds, and each radiates a different kind of power. Meter incites energy and focused attention, holding the musical mind captive. Tonality mesmerizes the musical mind, casting a kind of "magic spell" that enthralls the musical mind. Children's riveted attention to meter and to tonality often includes "deer-in-the-headlights" stares. Children's response to meter and to tonality leads one to believe that each resonates with something deep within that the children are fully wired for. Their spellbound attention to meter and to tonality appears as reverence for the art itself.

Meter and tonality activate wordless "contemplation" in the musical mind. Each stimulates the musical mind to "make sense," to create an "aural framework" for the understanding of rhythm and of melody—a sense of meter and a sense of tonality, which align respectively with the sound structures of meter and tonality.

The aural framework for rhythm is a kind of internal sound grid, within which rhythm falls into place. Ongoing immersion and interaction in a variety of meters leads the musical mind to discover differences in organizational schemes of beats, creating a non-verbal understanding of beat, the relationship between the large beats (macro beats) and the smaller beats (micro beats) in sound, and the differences across meters. This rich rhythm environment is without tonal (discreet pitches in relation to a tonal center), without words, and with movement.

The aural framework for tonal, independent of rhythm, is a kind of spatial sound-scape, in which pitches are received in relation to each other. Ongoing immersion and interaction in a variety of tonalities leads the musical mind to discover resting tone, pitches in relation to resting tone, and differences across tonalities. This rich tonal environment is without words, with movement, and with rhythm. Tonal, though independent of rhythm, is best learned with simple rhythm in the context of tonality. The musical mind attends to tonal more when it is presented in an easy meter with the simplest of rhythms than it does with tonal patterns without rhythmic definition.[1] More complex rhythms presenting tonality distract the musical mind from tonality, drawing attention to rhythm more than to tonality.[2]

The process of developing a sense of meter and a sense of tonality awakens and empowers children's artistry. The art itself draws children into sheer musicality. The developing sense of meter blooms into rhythmic precision in any meter, steady tempo, momentum in performance, and articulation, aligning the body with the musical mind's growing sense of meter. A sense of tonality blooms into tunefulness, singing in tune in any tonality, tone quality, and expression of line, aligning the voice with the musical mind's growing sense of tonality, and laying the groundwork for harmony. The process of developing a sense of meter and a sense of tonality provides the foundation for choral artistry.

## Uncommon Sense

Many common activities in our field thought to lead children to rhythmicity and tunefulness speak to the thinking mind. Some that attempt to address the musical mind do not offer sufficient "sound material" for the musical mind to grow on. Some teach beat and pitch as something external—that beat is something to watch or pitch something to match. A sense of beat and a sense of pitch have to come from within, and it is up to us as music teachers to teach the musical mind in its native language—meter and tonality, without words and with movement, so that children can generate rhythmicity and tunefulness by their own power.

Children who are already tuneful and rhythmic are not beyond the need for the "sound environment" of meters and tonalities. Being tuneful and rhythmic does not necessarily mean that the children have developed a sense of meter and a sense of tonality. All ages and stages benefit from experience with a variety of meters and tonalities, as it seats the sense of meter and sense of tonality, wherever they might be in process, producing more precise rhythmic performance and more in-tune tonal performance at all levels of development.

Our own thinking minds may lead us to believe that children would not attend to a musical narrative without words, props, or some kind of gimmick that draws them. Meter and tonality are the gimmicks. Meter and tonality provide the rhythm and tonal narratives, each of which takes the musical imagination on a new, exciting adventure with its own twists and turns that create line, movement, and expression. Each musical narrative compels the musical mind like a good story compels the thinking mind, focusing children's attention. The greater the immersion in the various meters and tonalities, the more artistry awakens, the more focused children's attention becomes, and the longer children attend to meter and to tonality.

The musical mind attends most to the uncommon meters and tonalities. Duple meter and Major tonality are so constant in our society that they do not awaken the musical mind. Ongoing engagement with the less common meters—Triple, Unusual Paired, and Unusual Unpaired meters, and the less common tonalities—Dorian, Mixolydian, Phrygian, Lydian, Aeolian, and Minor tonalities, lead the musical mind to perceive the unique relationships that define meter and tonality.[3] The broad experience with meter and tonality then leads the musical mind to receive Duple as a meter and Major as a tonality, rather than as the backdrop of society. (See Appendix A for the various meters and tonalities used in this book.)

Regular immersion in the variety of meters, accompanied by flowing movement, with opportunity for macro and micro beat movement, however imprecise it might be in the children, engages the body in making sense of meter—a sense of meter. Chants in the various meters, delivered on a neutral syllable through multiple successive repetitions, provide for immersion in meter. Figure 1.1 offers a chant in Triple meter, while Figure 1.2 presents one in Unusual Paired meter.

**Figure 1.1**
Triple

**Figure 1.2**
Unusual Paired

Regular immersion in the variety of tonalities, through singing and flowing movement, with opportunity for singing the resting tone, however imprecise it might be sung by the children, engages the body in making sense of tonality—a sense of tonality. Songs in the various tonalities, sung on a neutral syllable through multiple successive repetitions, provide for immersion in tonality. Figure 1.3 presents a song for immersion in Dorian tonality and Duple meter. Figure 1.4 presents one in Mixolydian tonality and Triple meter.

**Figure 1.3**
Dorian, Duple

**Figure 1.4**
Mixolydian, Triple

Engaging with the full variety of meters and tonalities develops a sense of meter and a sense of tonality far more than experience with just two contrasting meters or two contrasting tonalities. The greater diversity in meters and tonalities leads the musical mind to explore relationships in sound, much as toddlers explore stacking cups, eventually discovering relative size, color, and how they fit together. The musical mind's wordless exploration across meters leads children to discover in sound what a beat is, how macro and micro beats relate to each other, and how groupings of macro and micro beats in one meter are different from those of another, yet similar in function. The musical mind's wordless exploration across tonalities leads children to discover in sound the properties of resting tone, how pitches relate to that resting tone, and how they relate differently, yet similarly, in each tonality.

The musical mind's wordless exploration, discovery, and understanding of sound relationships is all part of the musical mind's way of knowing. Our attempts to get the thinking mind to articulate the knowing of the musical mind are no more "sound" than the thinking mind's recitation of note names or time values as an indicator of the musical mind's wordless knowing. The musical mind and the thinking mind will work together at a later point in time, but children's artistry is rooted in the non-verbal musical mind. It is imperative that we as music teachers and choral conductors reach and teach the musical mind, implementing wordless meters, tonalities, and movement to awaken and empower children's artistry.

## Budding Choral Artists

The musical mind under the spell of tonality is enthralled by art song that arises out of the tonal narrative. Going from pure tonality to art song in the same tonality evokes a kind of spiritual awe from children, as the musical mind meets the choral art.

Children engage in art song in the various tonalities with the reverence of choral artists. The power of tonality is so strong that art song arising out of tonal narrative is irresistible to children of all ages and stages who are engaged in its tonality, with the most uncommon tonalities initially being the most compelling. The "sound environment" of the overpowering tonality becomes an aural play space, within which children's artistry can explore the choral art through singing and movement, building and shaping lines, playing with momentum, the energy of the line, and the interaction between rhythm, melody, and text, without the interruption of the thinking mind.

The words of art song arising out of tonal narrative speak to the musical mind as sound, as a musical element in the combination of rhythm, melody, and text, rather than

**12**

as words that interrupt the musical mind and bring the thinking mind to the forefront. Children of all ages, like poets, savor the sound of the words, their rhythm and melody, and their interplay between rhythm and melody.

Art songs that most effectively serve to propel the children from tonality into the choral art are very short songs in the various tonalities, with texts that have their own artistic integrity, with rhythm that expresses the text very naturally in the meter or meters appropriate to the text, and with pure tonality and melodic line that serve the expression of text. These little art songs, through multiple repetitions, give children the opportunity to "practice" being choral artists, as they explore musical nuance in singing and movement.

**Figure 1.5**
Aeolian, Multimetric—
Duple/Triple

# The Modest Violet

*The Modest Violet* (Figure 1.5), offers an example of a very short art song that draws children of all ages from tonal narrative directly into the choral art, accompanied only by movement. The text, translated from Japanese haiku, is set in Aeolian tonality, with meter changes that accommodate the text. The melody climbs with the expression of text, pausing to reflect on the beauty of the shy little violet, before resolving.

Children's artistry demonstrates that the experience of the short little art song growing out of tonal narrative is most effective, most compelling, and most musical when sung repeatedly through eight to twelve repetitions, with movement, without talking. Successive repetitions invite children to explore musical dimensions repeatedly through singing and movement, discovering the artistry in the song and in themselves. The experience is so highly musical that children don't want to "break the spell" when they have to let go of the exciting journey of the musical imagination, just as they don't want to let go of an exciting adventure of the imagination of the thinking mind.

Art songs that reach the musical mind allure artistry, whatever the age, just as lovely children's poems entice adults as well as children. This type of art song serves children of all ages. Transposed up a third, it makes a fine warm-up for any chorus, as it engages the musical mind, body, and voice with the materials of the choral art in miniature, awakening artistry in all dimensions. (Additional little art songs in the various tonalities and meters are included in the Etudes, as are songs and chants for tonal and rhythm narratives.)

Songs for children are often chosen for their words rather than their musicality—words that appeal to the thinking mind. Focusing on words to teach the songs puts the thinking mind at the forefront. Tonal narrative puts the musical mind in charge.

A developing sense of meter and sense of tonality provide the readiness for children's artistry. Art songs in the various tonalities and meters can then transport children directly into the choral art, offering intimate experience with the musical materials of the choral art and laying the foundation for choral artistry.

# 2

# Moving Artistry

Movement embodies artistry. It enhances music learning. It propels artistry physically, developmentally, and spiritually. Movement offers a window into children's artistry, unveiling its wonder. Movement mirrors the art itself, making all dimensions of the choral art more tangible.

Movement speaks directly to the musical mind engrossed in meter or tonality. It is our most effective and most musical means of communicating with the musical mind in the context of music. Much of what we have tried to teach through words in our classrooms can be communicated non-verbally, more efficiently, and far more musically through movement.

Children's artistry urges us to expand our common notions about movement in the music classroom and children's chorus. Prescribed movement to song words, body percussion, dance, choreography, or choralography are only the tip of the iceberg. Children's artistry teaches us that movement that speaks to the musical mind in the context of meter or tonality most develops children's artistry, revealing artistry even before tunefulness and rhythmicity take hold.

We often assume that movement is essential to rhythm development, but it also plays a major role in tonal development. Movement mobilizes both rhythm and tonal knowing. It stimulates breath, momentum, physical support and energy for singing as well as for rhythmic delivery. The interplay between muscles and breath in movement are akin to the interplay between muscles and breath in both singing and rhythmic performance.[1] Movement is the vehicle that transports rhythm and tonal knowing from the musical mind to the body. It is the process through which rhythm knowing learns to align with the body to produce rhythmic performance, and the process through which tonal knowing learns to align with the body to produce tuneful singing.

We might assume that movement is most appropriate for very young children, yet movement does wonders to advance artistry with all ages and stages, including college choral ensembles. Perhaps we hesitate to use movement with older children because the judgmental thinking mind might balk at movement, which it may do when the musical mind is not engaged. Perhaps we have talked to the thinking mind about movement, directing the body to engage in Laban effort elements or stylistic movement, without ever having engaged the musical mind. Movement, without words, speaks directly to the musical mind compelled by meter or tonality, literally setting the musical mind in motion.

*Giving Voice to Children's Artistry.* Mary Ellen Pinzino, Oxford University Press. © Oxford University Press 2022.
DOI: 10.1093/oso/9780197606520.003.0003

We may be concerned that giving older students or choruses the freedom to move will lessen discipline, yet the musical mind focused by meter or tonality is highly disciplined, and its expression in movement heightens that focus. We might be concerned that movement will diminish vocal technique, yet appropriate movement can enhance vocal technique, often producing a sound and musicality not achieved by traditional means. The more we use movement in our teaching, whatever the age or context, the more musical our classrooms and choruses become, the more musical our teaching becomes, and the more transparent children's artistry becomes.

## Going with the Flow

We often assume that movement on the beat is prime, but flowing movement is even more basic. It is the movement between the beats. It is the blank canvas upon which we place weight and organize time, giving rise to beat and to meter. Flowing movement, in the context of the "sound environment" of meter and tonality, activates children's artistry. Meter and tonality stir the musical mind, while sustained, flowing movement engages the body, providing a vehicle for mobilization and expression of the musical mind.

Flowing movement is one of the most basic, yet most developed musical responses, exposing musicality in both the novice and the professional musician. It is highly musical and embodies momentum. Flowing movement becomes one with the flow of music like raindrops in a river, twisting, turning, and moving with the current.

The most effective and most musical flowing movement engages the whole body—extending arms in space, activating hips, shoulders, and knees, with feet planted firmly on the floor and the rest of the body in motion throughout the entire musical experience. Engaging in sustained, flowing movement with meters and tonalities may require breaking out of old practices and habitual conducting patterns. It may be a challenge not to succumb to pulse. Flowing movement is momentum between and through the beats without the imposition of weight or measurement of time.

Flowing movement may feel much the same across rhythm and melody and across different styles and tempos. Music flows, whether rhythm or melody, whatever the style or tempo. Sustained, flowing movement reflects the flow of music while giving body to the musical mind's processing of rhythm and tonal.

A teacher engaged in flowing movement—freely activating arms, hips, knees, and shoulders—becomes an invitation for children to do the same, communicating nonverbally the freedom to express and explore the wonder of the music. It conveys the important message that there is no right or wrong way to move, and demonstrates sheer musicality. Children's flowing movement in response communicates the depth of children's artistry.

## Weighty Issues

Flowing movement in the context of meter prepares the musical mind to take notice of the placement of weight within flow, giving rise to beat. The musical mind, attending to beats in relation to each other, discovers that beats are generally grouped by weight in twos or threes, that macro beats carry more weight than micro beats, and that melodic rhythm is in relation to macro and micro beats. The weighted grouping of beats defines meter.

The musical mind with a developed sense of meter not only understands beat groupings and weight distribution, but it is also "mindful" of both macro beats and micro beats simultaneously. Macro beats without micro beats result in a rushed tempo, as it is the pacing of micro beats within macro beats that secures tempo. Micro beats without macro beats do not define meter, as without the greater weight of macro beats there are no groupings since all beats sound alike. The presence of both macro beats and micro beats in the musical mind provides for the body and voice to execute meter precisely, whatever the meter.[2]

Movement with macro beats and with micro beats in the various meters provides opportunity for the musical mind to "practice" aligning the body with the musical mind, giving body to a sense of meter. Movement makes macro and micro beats tangible, and it offers a window to children's development of a sense of meter. The greater the interaction with macro beats and micro beats in the various meters, the stronger the developing sense of meter becomes and the more the musical mind and body become one.

Movement with macro beats and micro beats should reflect the contrast in weight between the two, whatever the meter. This contrast is essential to musical delivery and quality performance. The difference between performing macro and micro beats at the right time and performing them at the right time with appropriate weight distribution is the difference between accurate performance and highly musical performance. Figure 2.1 presents two measures of macro and micro beats in Duple meter, Triple meter, and Unusual Paired meters, with arrows indicating the weight of macro beats in each meter. (See Appendix B for weight distribution with additional beat groupings in unusual meters used in this book.)

**Figure 2.1**
Duple, Triple, Unusual Paired, macro beat weight

We sometimes think that because beat seems so obvious, or because children can easily "pick up the beat" with popular music in Duple meter, that the children are secure rhythmically. Seeming competence in Duple meter is regularly accompanied by lack of competence in Triple meter, even with experienced students. Tempos in Triple meter are often rushed, as micro beats are not paced or weighted in relation to macro beats. The greater the experience with macro and micro beats in unusual meters, the more secure the musical mind and body become in Duple and Triple meters as well as the unusual meters.

Rhythmic body alignment with the musical mind takes time and considerable experience with macro and micro beat movement in Duple, Triple, Unusual Paired, and Unusual Unpaired meters. Discussion about macro and micro beats does not shortcut the process, as the musical mind's understanding of macro beats and micro beats is in sound and movement rather than in words. Chanting in the various meters provides the "sound environment" for rhythmic movement, while the contrast between movement with macro beats and movement with micro beats speaks to the musical mind and to the body.

Alternating phrases of macro beat movement and micro beat movement demonstrates and reinforces the contrast between the two in each meter. Movement to both macro beats and micro beats simultaneously, with appropriate weight, provides for the musical mind to "practice" being mindful of both macro beats and micro beats at the same time.

Some types of macro and micro beat movement are far more effective than others in aligning the body with the developing sense of meter. Movement that uses full body weight is most effective. Standing and shifting weight side-to-side with macro beats uses body weight to reflect the weight of macro beats. Bending knees in an ongoing bounce with micro beats provides for the contrast in weight between macro and micro beats. The simultaneous shifting of weight on macro beats and bouncing on micro beats provides for appropriate weight distribution, with the heavier weight on macro beats created by both the full body shift of weight and the bounce into it.

The contrast between movement that uses full body weight for macro and micro beats and movement like clapping, stamping, or playing percussion instruments, is striking in terms of aligning the body with rhythm knowing. The smaller motor movements serve for children to explore knowing of the thinking mind or to apply an already developed sense of meter. They do not, however, teach the body to align with the musical mind in the development of a sense of meter. Full body weight most efficiently leads the body to become one with rhythm knowing.

The embodiment of rhythm knowing can be enhanced by adding "tonguing" to full body weight movement—"tonguing" an occasional unvoiced phrase of macro beats on an aspirated "too," contrasted by "tonguing" a phrase of micro beats, all with full body weight movement. The body musculature tends to follow the tongue.[3] The contrast between moving macro and micro beats with tonguing and then without tonguing helps the body to orchestrate the musical mind's understanding of macro and micro beats.

The most potent movement to align the musical mind, body, and spirit in macro and micro beat movement in the context of chant is leaping into macro beats while lively stepping micros. The thrust of full body weight applied to macro beats with lesser weight applied to micro beats brings the body and musical mind in sync most powerfully. Each meter presents a different challenge. A child delights in being able to navigate an unusual meter with this movement much as when first successful in jumping rope turned by peers. Using this "fancy footwork" with chant in a different meter each class session serves as a wonderful warm-up for choruses, including very developed ensembles. It activates the musical mind, engages the body with the musical mind, charges energy, takes singers out of where they were prior to rehearsal, and stimulates presence of the whole being in the process of making exciting music.

The embodiment of a sense of meter through macro and micro beat movement propels tonal development as well as rhythm development. The structure of a melodic line as it defines tonality, with its inherent relevance of resting tone and pitches in relation to resting tone, regularly aligns with the weight of macro and micro beats, reinforcing tonality in the musical mind. Flowing movement seems to simulate the "aural framework" that the musical mind develops in processing tonality, while weighted, meter movement makes it more tangible.

Body weight can be used directly to further embody tonal knowing. Engaging children in an occasional squat to sing the resting tone within tonal narrative makes resting tone more tangible and reinforces resting tone in sound, using body weight to mirror the weighted relevance of the resting tone. Using body weight on occasion for jumping while singing engages the breath and musculature for tuneful and supported singing. Children who have had considerable immersion in various tonalities, but who are not yet tuneful, often pop into tuneful singing while jumping.[4] The tone of an ensemble of tuneful singers often soars when the children are jumping while singing. Both instances provide children with the experience of what it "feels like" to energize the breath and musculature for full-bodied singing, which can then transfer to energy in vocal production without jumping.[5]

The body learns to deliver what the musical mind knows rhythmically and tonally through full body movement. Flowing movement and weighted movement offer the catalyst for rhythm knowing to bloom into precise rhythm performance and for tonal knowing to bloom into tuneful and in-tune singing.

## Moving into the Choral Art

Children with substantial experience in both flowing and weighted movement in the context of meter and tonality engage in a highly musical manner with art song that grows out of tonality. Children literally become the song, expressing in singing and movement the energy of the line, embracing every musical nuance that is pushing and pulling that energy. The soundscape, through successive repetitions of the art song, becomes a sandbox of musical energy within which children explore musical nuance and repeatedly build lines, turn phrases, create contrast, and articulate text in singing and movement, enacting a "play" of energy, with each child as director and the lyrics as script.

Movement is the "sign language" of the musical mind, through which all dimensions of artistry and the choral art can be communicated. Movement makes all aspects of music more tangible. It gives singers the opportunity to "feel" the musical import in all its nuance, prompted by their own musical imaginations and the choral art itself. Children revel in their own artistry and in its interaction with the choral art. They unveil, in the process, sheer musicality and the sheerness—the transparency—of children's artistry.

Movement mirrors music in all dimensions, providing a vehicle for generating line, phrasing, dynamics, and momentum in singers that is inherent in the music. It also mirrors children's artistry, demonstrating children's command of the music, individually and in ensemble. Each child's movement while singing is a visual indication of the child's level of mastery with each aspect of the song being rehearsed in movement, guiding the teacher to better reach the musical needs of the individual, as well as the ensemble. The visual "printout" that movement provides of each individual's and the ensemble's concept of the music offers a fine diagnostic tool, guiding the teacher to demonstrate movement that better captures the musical needs of the music.

Movement embodies tone, articulation, line, phrasing, dynamics, expression, and style, as well as a sense of meter and a sense of tonality. Every movement the body makes, the voice follows. Movement is the finest accompaniment to singing, and the key to unlocking children's artistry. Music moves. Musicians move. Choral sound moves. Musical movement transports singers to richer tone, greater focus, and greater artistry, when we engage the musical mind and embody its brilliance in movement.

Teachers as well as children become more musical in movement. There are far more musical aspects of the choral art to conduct than beats. Movement between the beats, flow, weight, momentum, line, expression, and articulation can all be expressed and demonstrated in movement. Arms, hips, knees, and shoulders in sustained movement can reflect all dimensions of the choral art. Flowing movement can capture line, ongoing momentum, and expression. Weighted movement carries meter and energy. Arms and hands can articulate text with such precision that the voice has no choice but to execute such musicality. Teacher and singers, together, in movement, become a community of artists making exciting music.

## Getting the Picture

You might prefer to view videos demonstrating children's artistry in movement rather than reading about it, but that would deprive you of insights to be gained by your own experimentation and discovery of the power of movement in your own classroom. The children have much to teach you about movement that will be far more meaningful than trying to imitate a video. They will take you beyond any limitations or insecurities you might feel about movement with their creativity and freedom to move. Children engaged in their own artistry will naturally generate movement that captures this or that musical nuance that you couldn't quite find in your own body, clarifying and showing you what you were wanting to communicate in movement.

You will hear the difference in the sound of your ensemble when your singers are engaged in movement. You will feel the difference in momentum in song when the children deliver in meter with appropriate weight distribution. You will discover that movement draws artistry out of every singer; that it levels the broad range of skills within the group, propelling less experienced singers to higher levels of musicality; and that rhythms and lines that seemed out of reach often clear up with movement. You will discover how much musicality movement can communicate that words cannot, and how the muscles remember what might otherwise be forgotten. You will sense the difference in energy in your classroom when singers are moving—both musical energy and exuberance for making exciting music.

Experiment with movement in your classroom. Start by adding movement to already established practices just to witness its impact on sound, energy, vocal technique, and musicality. Invite movement in a song the children already know and see what you learn. Explore flowing movement in a song and then weighted movement in the same song. Sustain movement throughout successive repetitions, going from flowing movement to weighted movement, to something that reflects the energy of the line, dynamics, or articulation. Draw from all kinds of movement to most reflect and best demonstrate your desired execution of the song and see how it might change children's delivery.

Introduce a new song, inviting children to move with you as you sing through multiple repetitions, asking them to start singing when they are ready. Movement offers the most immediate access to music. Experiencing the song first in movement gives singers a "feel" for style, mood, meter, tempo, contrasts, the energy of the line, and the interaction between rhythm, melody, and text, making words, rhythm, and melody much easier to grasp.

Try some of your favorite choral warm-ups with movement and see what you discover. Try applying movement to particular challenges you have encountered. Invite singers to literally step into a line and you'll hear the difference in sound and energy. Try using deep knee bends or full body arm thrusts with ascending or descending lines and notice how it does or doesn't affect delivery. Try experimenting in front of a mirror until you find the movement that reflects your musical intent. Have singers take a step back with a decrescendo, or place the end of a phrase gently on an imaginary table with arms and hands. Request that they throw shoulders into a building line or use arms and shoulders to shape or reach the peak of a phrase. Capture articulation in arms and hands in ensemble and listen to the clear execution of voices. Ask the singers to hold hands while singing and watch the energy pumping through a more musical execution.

Use words wisely with any movement request, so that thinking minds do not take over. Wordy descriptions, invitations for individual demonstrations, or even praise can get in the way of the musical mind. Movement bypasses the thinking mind. It frees the musical mind and body to work in tandem without the judgmental thinking mind. Movement circumvents self-consciousness and, with an awakened musical mind, displaces and overcomes it.

Play with movement in your classroom. There is no right or wrong way to move and no right or wrong application of movement. The musical needs of the singers and the musical needs of the songs will guide you in applying movement in the choral rehearsal, and the outcome you experience with each application will teach you to use movement more effectively in rehearsal. We will always be students of movement, just as we will always be students of music. Every piece of music moves and each offers a different challenge in movement, providing an opportunity for us to better understand the art—and its movement.

Music and movement are inseparable. You, like the children, will grow to make movement and singing inseparable. Lines, phrases, and passages rehearsed in movement engrave musicality into singers' delivery. The body remembers what the thinking mind forgets and won't deliver the line or phrase that was rehearsed sufficiently with movement without the "feeling" that goes with it. Singers become so musical in movement that they do not sing without it—without musicality.

Movement can be applied to every dimension of the choral art—line, phrasing, dynamics, articulation, enunciation, attacks, releases. Every musical nuance can be manifest in movement. Every movement generates the corresponding nuance in vocal delivery. Every application of movement energizes singers and awakens artistry in the choral rehearsal.[6]

# Breathing Life into Vocal Technique

Movement can facilitate the development of all dimensions of vocal technique. It stimulates breath, support, head voice, resonance, and energy—all in the context of musicality. Movement activates the whole musculature for singing. Children lost in their own artistry with appropriate movement in the delivery of a line cannot sing it without breath, support, and energy. Taking sufficient breath becomes more the embodiment of the musical mind than something the thinking mind has to remember. Movement generates breath, with singers taking sufficient breath for whatever line they are delivering in movement and singing.

The many requests to singers to use a head voice, think high, support the sound, breathe from the diaphragm, open the palate, support the upper torso, stand tall, and drop the jaw are not necessary when we engage singers in movement.

Vocal production is in the domain of the body, yet we have traditionally addressed it intellectually. The whole body is the vocal instrument. The mechanics of singing can only be imagined. Movement makes vocal technique more tangible, communicating non-verbally to the whole body—relieving tension, developing tone, breath, vowel placement, and resonance. Full body movement that opens the arms opens the sound. Movement that actively engages knees evokes appropriate breath. Arm movement that generates energy while singing in the high register, assures space in the sound. The physical experience of good vocal production stimulated by movement teaches the muscles far more effectively and efficiently than the intellectualization of the vocal process.[7]

Movement puts the focus on musicality, with vocal technique in its rightful place as subordinate to musicality rather than the generating force. Even college students without musical backgrounds can develop appropriate vocal technique through movement that reflects the musical import of the music. The more we explore the power of movement on the voice with all ages, the more we secure vocal technique and the less we have to rely on traditional practices to improve vocal production.

Warm-ups employed for vocal technique become far more musical with movement, stimulating deliberate musicality with each ongoing repetition rather than automatic routine. Stepping forward and opening arms while singing a five-note ascending pattern, stepping backward and lowering arms while singing the descending pattern give shape, phrasing, and musical meaning to the warm-up, making each half-step higher repetition more musical than the last. Deep knee bends with arms close to the body while singing a pitch, opening to upright, reaching movement with full extended arms while singing the octave higher gives breadth in sound and expression to successive jumps of an octave, returning to the starting position to approach the next octave a half-step higher.

Engaging the musical mind with tonality in movement makes warm-ups even more meaningful. Traditional warm-ups can be set in different tonalities. Short art songs that grow out of tonality give singers experience with the various dimensions of the choral art that can then transfer to much more difficult choral material. Art songs that invite the delivery of expressive line, momentum, articulation, and contrast through singing and movement warm up the musical mind, the voice, and the body, developing vocal technique, greater musicality, and choral artistry.

> Singers become more focused on the production of sound through movement than they do by trying to will the muscles to obey. The kinesthetic sense of sound and vocal production stimulated by movement becomes the template for singing with good vocal technique, which can then be triggered in any piece of choral literature through movement.[8]

## Moving Energy

Energy is the life force of choral artistry. It is energy that moves the breath, moves the line, and moves the soul. Singing without that life force is boring—for the singers and for the audience. Music comes alive when the energy of the life force and the energy of the line come together. Movement that expresses musical nuance ignites that fusion.

We often resort to an upbeat song, clever words, or stepping and clapping to enliven or motivate our children. Yet movement that captures musical import, whatever the style or tempo, mobilizes both the energy of the life force and the energy of the line. It is musicality that energizes and motivates singers.

We often become so concerned that singers get the right notes at the right time with the right words, that we forget about the vibrance that makes choral singing exciting— for singers and for the audience. We can place such a high priority on achieving a rich sound that we forget the importance of rhythmic energy, momentum, and vitality. Beautiful tone, accurate rhythm, and quality repertoire do not make up for a lack of life energy in singers; nor does proper decorum or singing posture. We must actively cultivate the energy of the life force in our singers and bring it together with the energy of the line.

The very act of moving generates energy, enlivens rehearsals, makes singing and rehearsing more playful, and diminishes talking—both students' and teachers'. Communicating and enacting the energy of the line through movement leaves very little for teachers to "talk about." Focused musical minds engaged in musical delivery are excited rather than bored, more anxious to make delivery even more musical than to be derailed by the thinking minds of peers.

Musical energy dominates the classroom, sidelining the thinking mind. Sustaining that energy through movement allows the occasional verbal suggestion from the teacher to be received without thinking minds taking over. Movement creates energy, picking up the pacing of rehearsals, making musicality highly compelling, with fewer gaps of dead energy that diminish the life force necessary for making exciting music.

Engaging singers in movement serves yet another role in energizing the life force. It transfers the power of the podium to the singers, stimulating greater deliberateness, expression, and confidence from each singer, greater individual responsibility for making exciting music, and greater ownership of both the process and the product. Movement empowers singers with their own artistry.

## Moving Rehearsals

Movement is our greatest resource to improve performance in the choral rehearsal. We can apply movement to every musical challenge that needs rehearsal. One passage or song might need work on meter, articulation, or vocal technique, whereas another needs direct attention on expression, tempo, or dynamics. The key is for conductor and singers to stay in motion. Demonstrate the movement that best captures your desired outcome. Movement applied to any dimension of the choral art teaches the body what it "feels like" to execute that aspect of the music as intended. Focusing on macro and micro beat weight distribution within the context of a song, for example, better assures that appropriate weight distribution will be sustained when not directly attending to weight. Muscles remember that "rehearsed feeling" within the delivery of the greater whole.

**WHAT DOES LITTLE BIRDIE SAY?**

**Figure 2.2**

Dorian, Multimetric—
Duple/Triple

Assume that you are going to teach **What Does Little Birdie Say?** (Figure 2.2), with the lovely poetry of Alfred Lord Tennyson, to a group of tuneful third graders who have had extensive experience in the various meters and tonalities. This song is in Dorian tonality, which in itself will grab the attention of the musical mind, and it shifts back and forth between Duple and Triple meter, increasing the musical difficulty and the interest of the musical mind. Vocally, the range is appropriate for children's voices, and the placement of the song within that range promotes proper use of voice and appropriate vocal technique.[9] The delightful words of Alfred Lord Tennyson present three distinct characters—a narrator, a little bird wanting to fly, and a protective mother bird—offering an interesting challenge in expression.

Start with a Dorian narrative to seat children in Dorian tonality for the new song. Shift resting tone if necessary, set up Dorian in the new key, and then sing the song with full body movement, capturing the style, tempo, meter changes, the drama of the text, and the energy of the line in both song and movement. Invite the children to move with you and then to sing when they are ready. Successive repetitions provide for children to explore the song's musicality, expression, and drama in movement, whether or not they are yet singing. Notice their capture of the dramatic contrasts in this song in both singing and movement, reflecting your expression of intensity and leaning into ascending lines.

Use arms and hands to capture articulation of the sections in Duple meter, while knees and hips articulate meter. Shift to more flowing movement in the arms and shoulders in the sections in Triple meter, with knees and hips articulating the new meter, capturing the difference in style between the little bird's need for independence and the mother's determined protection. Notice your own movement as you take a breath for each phrase and how movement in the context of musicality cues breath. The more you become one with the song in singing and movement, the more children will become the song.

Take a moment before we go on with rehearsal to consider how much you have communicated to your students in this short time without interrupting musicality with words. You have secured tonality, promoting in-tune singing. You have pointed out the shifting meters, without talking about them, and communicated the ongoing pulsing of both macro and micro beats in the contrasting meters, as well as the consistency of micro beats across meters, all in the context of musicality. You have sparked intrigue with the opening question with energy and expression. You have addressed the difference in style and articulation between the opening and the little bird's longing, and again between the anxious mother and the little bird's triumph. You have communicated flow, weight, momentum, tempo, articulation, the rhythm of the melody and its precision within the shifting meters. You have taught the melody and the text, with its inherent expression. You have naturally demonstrated appropriate breath, including perhaps a catch breath in the middle of the second phrase, articulating the bird's plea. You have enacted the energy of the line, culminating with the drama of the final measures. You have communicated full expressive import and the sustaining of exciting delivery throughout.

The children's execution of this song in singing and movement after such a short time can only be musical, with melody, rhythm, and text intact, and tempo and intonation secured, all with appropriate articulation, expression, and vital energy. You haven't talked about anything. You have simply engaged in singing and movement throughout the encounter and invited the children to do the same. Contrast such a musical interchange with your students with using language to address musicality in singing this song. Contrast the interest and attention of the children learning this song through singing and movement with the belabored teaching of song words, vocal technique, pitches, and correct rhythm without movement and without the context of tonality and meter. Note the energy in the classroom, the pacing of the rehearsal, and the children's excitement for this song in such a musical context. The children's artistry will move you just as your artistry has moved them, as you work together as a community of artists, making exciting music.

This musical interaction was just the children's first encounter with this song. It could serve as an experience within itself. It could serve as a choral warm-up, engaging the musical mind, body, and spirit with the choral art. It could serve as the initial experience with a song intended for choral performance with piano accompaniment.

Let's assume that your intent is to prepare this piece for performance in the next concert. Identify what needs rehearsal and apply movement. Children with a background in meters and tonalities generally won't have a problem with the shifting meters or intonation. Whatever might be lacking in delivery can guide you to foundational needs as well as whatever might need greater rehearsal. Insecurity in meter indicates the need for greater experience with both Duple and Triple meters in chant with movement, contrasted by unusual meters. Rushed tempos most often indicate the lack of micro beats within meter and the lack of appropriate weight distribution between macro and micro beats. Lack of momentum might suggest the need for greater experience with flowing movement, or the need for greater weight on the macro beats.

Intonation problems generally arise from lack of experience with the various tonalities in flowing movement. Greater experience with all tonalities leads children to sing this song with the "mindset" of Dorian in the musical mind, rather than the more familiar Major, securing intonation. Greater energy in movement that generates breath might also fix an intonation problem, as might engaging knees with upper torso movement. This song's placement in the child voice diminishes issues with vocal technique.[10] Movement in itself will likely take care of tone, breath, and support, with perhaps a bit of tweaking of vowel coloring to reach the desired effect.

Problems with articulation or diction of text can usually be fixed by rehearsing articulation of text in movement. Arms and hands that capture the desired outcome will bring the voice right along with it. The issue could be rooted in a more basic lack of a developing sense of meter, needing experience in both flowing and weighted movement in a variety of meters. Then the rhythm of the line, and hence the text, will fall into place in the musical mind and body.

Lines delivered without expression or energy will improve when movement reflects the desired expression or energy of those lines. Dynamics rehearsed with movement will produce the contrast you seek. This song captures the expression of text in all its drama, so that rehearsing through singing and movement will deliver the expression of text with its inherent conflict between the little bird and mother, with the increased tension created by the narrator.

Targeted rehearsal to achieve greater nuance with a particular pitch, entrance, end of phrase, or other aspect of musical performance can also be enhanced through movement. Find in your own body what you seek in expression and you will be able to communicate it to your singers. Greater urgency in the opening question, for example, could result from being on the balls of the feet and leaning in slightly while bouncing micro beats. Greater distinction between the characters of narrator, bird, and mother can be achieved by literally stepping into each different role. Greater breath, support, energy, or drama in the delivery of the final two measures might be achieved by rehearsing the line with engaged knees, using outstretched arms to wind up energy to the peak of the song, or stepping forward with each of the three pitch levels. The desired effect may be found in a combination of these options, something you discovered in front of a mirror, or movement you saw in a child.

Adding the complexity of piano accompaniment may require additional rehearsal on some of these same issues, now with piano accompaniment. Tempo, momentum, articulation, and expression can all be better secured with movement, with or without piano accompaniment. Only a bit of additional tweaking might be needed to then fully bring the song to performance level. (Piano accompaniment for this song can be found in the Come Children Sing Institute SONG LIBRARY at comechildrensing.com/sl.php.)

Can movement in rehearsal be applied similarly to more difficult music, singing in parts, and more developed singers? Absolutely! Add movement to rehearsal with any ensemble and watch artistry soar. Rehearsing with movement can improve performance at all levels. (See Etude 2 for the application of movement specifically to momentum and the energy of the line.)

Movement is inherent in all music. Embodiment of that movement propels musicality at all levels. College singers thrive on movement in rehearsal at their own level of choral literature and performance, as making exciting music is exciting for singers. Movement makes every aspect of the choral art come alive. The way vocal parts work together, imitate, or play off each other becomes more tangible in movement, whatever the complexity, with the independence, yet dependence upon each part for the greater whole.

## Moving Performance

Performance of world music and new compositions for children's chorus have given life to greater movement in choral performance, with choreography an integral part of the songs. More traditional performance practices present disciplined children's choruses standing still while singing, presuming that movement is distracting and takes away from quality performance. We take away far more from quality performance by restricting movement. Fidgeting distracts. Musical movement does not. Expecting singers to sing musically without movement is like expecting music to be musical without movement.

It is up to each of us to decide how to channel movement energy in performance. Overt movement in rehearsal naturally becomes more covert movement in performance, as singers generally tame movement in front of an audience. Some singers, however, depend on movement in performance to stave off the thinking mind's self-consciousness, and most all sing more musically with movement. Performance has to be imbued with the "feeling of movement" known in rehearsal, whether movement is overt or covert in concert.

Highly respected choruses have applied the musicality of movement with singing in various ways in concert. The internationally known high school men's chorus of St. Mary's International School in Japan, under the direction of Randy Stenson, performs with every singer conducting the musicality of his own part in concert. Their performance is remarkable. The well-known St. Olaf College Choir, under the direction of Anton Armstrong, holds hands in performance, joyfully bubbling with movement energy throughout their performance of Bach, inspiring both singers and audience by their moving performance. Anima Glen Ellyn Children's Chorus, performing under the direction of Emily Ellsworth with Chicago's Grant Park Symphony Orchestra, sang with such alert and vital energy throughout their part in Carmina Burana that one assumed the children to be in motion, even without the appearance of overt movement. The renowned Chicago Children's Choir and Vocality, the festival chorus of young adults, both under the direction of Josephine Lee, engaged in ongoing movement that was stunning in a performance of Bernstein's Mass with the Chicago Symphony Orchestra. The conducting-like movement of each singer, whether for theatrical effect or vocal execution, embodied musicality and was an essential part of their exemplary choral performance.

Music moves in performance, and so do our finest musicians. Yo-Yo Ma, as soloist with the Chicago Symphony Orchestra, dramatically engages in expressive movement throughout his entire performance. Movement of the principal clarinetist rows back reflects the musicality of every line he plays, while the eyebrows of a second violinist articulate lines along with the movement of her bow. Being a musician demands mastery of the movement of music.

Let us rethink old notions about stage presence so that we might channel movement energy in performance rather than restricting movement in concert and compromising children's artistry. Let us create "moving performance," with children delivering so musically that movement is palpable, whether overt or covert on stage.

# 3

# Inspiring Artistry

Children's artistry deserves songs that merit its wonder. It soars with songs that capture the musical mind, challenge and feed musicality, and spark excitement in the intertwining of rhythm, melody, and text. Children's artistry thrives on songs that arouse its poetic sense of words, release the inner child, and express children's artistry. It revels in songs that make the child voice ring, support vocal execution, and inspire children to sing beautifully.

Songs are the vehicle for the full expression of children's artistry in the music classroom and children's chorus. They are the means to reaching the musical mind, children's deep reservoir of expression, and the choral art. They serve both process and product. Well-chosen songs can stimulate, support, and develop children's artistry at every level.

Songs that captivate the musical mind propel artistry in flight. Song repertoire that does not compel the musical mind can cause it to quietly withdraw and shut down. The musical mind cannot communicate that this song is unmusical, that this song does not capture or challenge the musical mind, or that this song is way beyond its level of development. The musical mind registers its opinion by either engaging or withdrawing. It cannot help but come alive in songs that captivate the musical mind, and it cannot pretend to be enlivened in those that do not. Singing with appropriate pitches, note values, words, breath, and diction does not guarantee that children's artistry is engaged. The musical mind will often politely sit on the sidelines and let the thinking mind do what it is told—get louder here, take a breath there, articulate that "t." A child whose musical mind is not engaged in the music class is like a child whose thinking mind is not engaged in an academic class. Children with bored musical minds often become disruptive or want to quit chorus.

We all like to find songs that appeal to children, but are we wanting to appease the thinking mind or the musical mind? The judgmental thinking mind is quick to voice an opinion about song repertoire, favoring upbeat songs in Duple meter and Major tonality, with words that are clever, funny, or "cool." It likes songs that are immediate, with a strong beat and repetitive melody. The musical mind is mesmerized by songs in the various tonalities, with the more unusual tonalities the most compelling. The musical mind loves interesting rhythm that expresses text. It devours song words for their sound, rhythm, and melody that give depth to their meaning, and it basks in the delight of the intertwining of rhythm, melody, and text. The musical mind, like the thinking mind, might love an upbeat song with a strong beat and clever words, but only if the musicality

*Giving Voice to Children's Artistry.* Mary Ellen Pinzino, Oxford University Press. © Oxford University Press 2022.
DOI: 10.1093/oso/9780197606520.003.0004

of the song earns the attention of the musical mind. The participation of the musical mind is dependent upon the musicality of the song. The thinking mind becomes an enthusiastic partner when the musical mind is engaged.

Songs that give voice to children's artistry elicit the musicianship, expression, and sound needed to deliver the musicality inherent in each song. They ignite artistry within. They develop the readiness for more difficult song repertoire and motivate children to further engage with the choral art. They empower children with their own artistry, leading to exciting delivery that expresses the beauty of each song and the beauty of each child. *Songs that give voice to children's artistry draw artistry out of every child and draw every child into the choral art.*

## The Full Spectrum

Singing is universal. It is the expression of childhood; of children's artistry; of the child's mind, body, and spirit; and of the choral art, yet our field often views early childhood music, classroom music, and children's chorus as unrelated. The acquisition of musicianship with voice as the primary instrument presents a continuum of development throughout childhood. Giving voice to children's artistry is an ongoing process through all arbitrary divisions of early childhood, elementary, middle school, junior high, and beyond, or designations of classroom music and children's chorus.

Viewing the spectrum of development through the lens of age or context masks the need for continuity throughout. It also blinds us to the sameness in the process of developing artistry across ages and contexts. Teaching to the musical mind and developing a sense of meter and a sense of tonality are more alike at every level than they are different. Musical movement propels energy and artistry with all ages. Songs that inspire children's artistry are essential at every level. The process of giving voice to children's artistry is consistent, whatever the age or context, suggesting that we rethink some of our common practices.

We favor play with young children and serious artistry with select ensembles, yet musicality at all levels requires playfulness, and children of all ages are capable of artistry. We champion children's folk songs for young children and quality choral literature for advanced singers, but children's artistry exposes the need for songs that give voice to children's artistry at all ages and stages. Language educators provide quality literature of increasing difficulty throughout childhood, in addition to folk rhymes for young children and Shakespeare for older children. Instrumental music instruction offers continuity across all levels, with increasing difficulty throughout, assuring at every level the readiness for more advanced music making. We as a field now know enough about the process of music learning and the development of choral artistry that we can no longer overlook the need for continuity in the quality and difficulty progression of song literature for children of all ages and stages, whatever the methodology.

Children's artistry deserves increasingly difficult song repertoire at every level—songs that give voice to children's artistry and develop the readiness for more advanced song literature. The merit of songs for the development of children's artistry is not in their historical, cultural, or social considerations, but in their musical considerations that give rise to children's artistry.

Song, itself, directs artistry at every level. The properties of song and how they intertwine impact the musical mind, artistic expression, vocal technique, and ensemble sound. Children's artistry unfolds in songs that compel the musical mind, prompt artistic expression, and enable vocal technique—songs that inspire children's artistry.

## Song Architecture

The architecture of song—the way rhythm, melody, and text work independently and together in the expression of text—directly affects the musical mind, artistic expression, and vocal technique. Rhythm, melody, and text, though married in song, exert their independence through inherent difficulty factors in each, which are compounded by their interaction. Meter, tonality, melodic contour, the components of rhythm, the way rhythm and melody present themselves in song, and the way they work together all contribute to rhythm and tonal difficulty in the musical mind. The musical setting of text dictates yet complicates rhythmic and melodic difficulty factors and determines the difficulty of artistic expression. Vocal placement of the child voice in tandem with the rhythmic, melodic, and expressive realization of text determine the difficulty of vocal technique.

The architecture of songs that give voice to children's artistry scaffolds every dimension of developing artistry—the musical mind, artistic expression, and vocal technique—at every level, enabling artistry in all children, and propelling children into choral artists. This revelation came about through many years of research at the Come Children Sing Institute, which included extensive review and implementation of song repertoire with children of all ages and stages in both classroom and choral settings, plus the composing and field testing of hundreds of new songs for children at all levels. The long-term classroom research was informed by ongoing discoveries about the developing musical mind and the developing choral musician. Findings, presented here, address how song can support the musical mind, prompt artistic expression, and enable vocal technique in the development of children's artistry. They begin with a closer look at the properties of song in relation to how the musical mind responds in song, difficulty factors, and song architecture that supports children's developing artistry. Songs that were written and field tested as part of this research were integral to understanding its findings. Those presented here demonstrate the progression of children's artistry in song with children as young as five through advanced choristers.

## Rhythm

Song rhythm offers its own inherent difficulty, with or without melody and text. The musical mind in song contends with rhythm difficulty, plus the challenges created by rhythm's interaction with melody and text. Rhythm in song, separate from its intertwining with melody and text, is a major factor in song difficulty and the progression of increasing difficulty in song repertoire.

The difficulty of meters, beat functions, and patterns developed by Edwin Gordon are consistent in song, with or without words. Triple meter is more difficult than Duple meter. The unusual meters are more difficult than Duple and Triple meters. Shifting meters add greater challenge. Melodic rhythm patterns with macro and micro beats are the easiest in each meter, with macro beats alone more difficult than micro beats alone, and divisions of micro beats a greater challenge. (See Appendix A for macro beats, micro beats, and divisions.) Rhythm patterns that include elongations, rests, ties, and upbeats are considerably more challenging, with each function of increasing difficulty.[1] The rests and ties in Figure 3.1 present considerable difficulty in Duple meter. Figure 3.2 offers an example in the more difficult Triple meter, but with easier macro/micro beat patterns and divisions.

**Figure 3.1**
Duple with rests, ties, and upbeats

**Figure 3.2**
Triple with divisions

Songs that serve children's artistry clearly define and sustain meter. The relationship between macro and micro beats is established early in the song, whatever the meter, securing both meter and tempo in the musical mind. A developing sense of meter needs ongoing support in sound of the organization of beats that defines meter.

The rhythm in Figure 3.2 clearly establishes Triple meter, with the contrasting macro and micro beats in the first measure. The second and third measures offer a bit more challenge for the musical mind to hold on to Triple meter, with divisions in the second measure and only macro beats in the third measure. The fourth measure, which again presents the contrast between macro and micro beats, reinforces Triple meter in the musical mind. Figure 3.3, in contrast, does not establish Triple meter. The relationship between macro and micro beats in Triple meter is not offered in sound. Songs that do not present and sustain macro and micro beats in relation to each other are appropriate only after children have developed the more advanced rhythm skills of inferring and sustaining meter with appropriate weight distribution without direct support from the song itself.

**Figure 3.3**
Triple without meter definition

Songs that serve the development of children's artistry meet children's musical needs. They provide support for the musical mind at every level. Children with facility in Triple meter may be ready for a song with the underlying rhythm of Figure 3.2, but not nearly ready for that of Figure 3.3. A particularly fast or extremely slow tempo can affect rhythm difficulty, but children with the readiness for a song's meter and rhythm can generally handle that song at most any tempo. Establishing the meter and tempo with the children in sound, prior to singing a song, is helpful in securing meter at all levels of development, as is rehearsing a song with metric movement with appropriate weight distribution.

Assessing the rhythm difficulty of song guides us in choosing songs that are appropriate for our children's rhythm development. Knowing the difficulty inherent in rhythm also helps us to pinpoint problems in rehearsal with any song repertoire. Rhythm challenges are often masked as issues with text or articulation. Rhythm difficulty may explain why children can maintain a steady tempo in one song and not another; why they struggle with a particular entrance or passage; or why a song with a simple text might be harder to learn than one with a more difficult text.

## Tonal

Tonal, like rhythm, presents its own inherent difficulty, with or without rhythm or text. The musical mind in song contends with tonal difficulty in addition to rhythm difficulty, plus the challenges presented by tonal's intertwining with rhythm and text. The properties of tonal in song, separate from rhythm and text, affect the development of children's artistry.

Songs that serve children's artistry clearly establish and sustain tonality. A developing sense of tonality needs the ongoing support in song of the organization of pitches that defines tonality. Resting tone is the magnetizing force of tonality. The resting tone and fifth serve as tonal anchors in the musical mind, much as macro and micro beats serve as rhythm anchors. Tonal anchors, however, are the same across tonalities, unlike macro and micro beats which are unique to each meter. It is the particular combination of pitches in relation to the resting tone that identifies each tonality.

The Major scale in Figure 3.4 shares the same resting tone and fifth as the scale in Dorian tonality (Figure 3.5). The characteristic tones of Dorian that distinguish it from Major tonality are the lowered third and lowered seventh. Note that the sixth is the same as in Major, which distinguishes Dorian tonality from Aeolian, which includes a lowered third, lowered seventh, and lowered sixth.

**Figure 3.4**
Major

**Figure 3.5**
Dorian

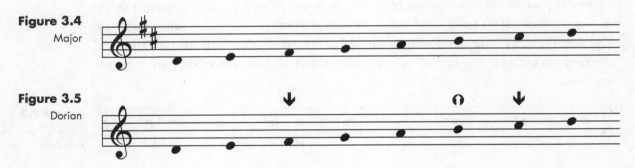

The characteristic tones of a tonality have to be present relatively early in a song and be included regularly to establish and sustain tonality. The characteristic raised fourth in Lydian tonality, for example, is unique to Lydian, and the only pitch that distinguishes Lydian from Major. (See Appendix C for characteristic tones of the various tonalities.)

Melodic contour also plays a role in establishing tonality. The melody in Figure 3.6 presents the characteristic raised fourth of Lydian tonality in both the second and third measures. The melodic contour, with its descending passage, also helps to secure Lydian in the musical mind, as the second occurrence of the raised fourth in the descending passage cues the musical mind to process the whole song in Lydian tonality rather than as Major with an accidental. The similar melody in Figure 3.7, without a hint of the raised fourth and with the ascending passage, leads the musical mind to process the melody in the more familiar Major tonality and sing the fourth flat as it would in F Major.

**Figure 3.6**
Lydian

**Figure 3.7**
Lydian, but misleading

The third, sixth, and seventh are the characteristic tones that distinguish one tonality from another, with the addition of the fourth in Lydian and the second in Phrygian. The establishment of tonality in the awakened musical mind can be done with fewer characteristic tones, provided that the tonality is unmistakably distinguished from the others. Mixolydian, for example, might be established by the inclusion of the third and seventh without the sixth, as it is the lowered seventh that distinguishes Mixolydian from Major (Figure 3.8). A melody with a minor third and lowered seventh without a sixth, however, could be either Dorian or Aeolian, so the sixth would have to be present along with the minor third and lowered seventh to define the tonality.

Phrygian tonality might be established in song with very few pitches, as in Figure 3.9, as only Phrygian has the minor second, and this example includes the lowered seventh as well. The combination of the minor second and lowered seventh in relation to the resting tone is unmistakably Phrygian. Note that Pentatonic, without a seventh or fourth, does not sufficiently define a tonality, so it does not serve in developing a sense of tonality. The Pentatonic melody in Figure 3.10 could be in Lydian, Mixolydian, or Major tonality.

**Figure 3.8**
Mixolydian

**Figure 3.9**
Phrygian

**Figure 3.10**
Pentatonic

Characteristic tones of a tonality, by themselves, are not sufficient to define or sustain tonality. Melodic contour, with abundant stepwise passages that spin off of and move to and from the resting tone and fifth, and that includes characteristic tones, draws the musical mind into tonality. The simple Dorian melody in Figure 3.11 exemplifies this contour and includes characteristic tones.

**Figure 3.11**
Dorian

Musical lines leading down to the tonic seem easier for children than those going up to the tonic. Songs with abundant stepwise passages that spin off of and move to and from the resting tone and fifth support the musical mind, whereas angular melodies are far more difficult. Children readily handle skips between tonic and dominant pitches, and then skips within the harmonic functions that uniquely define the tonality with its characteristic tones. (See Appendix D for harmonic functions that define the various tonalities.)

A song that begins and ends on the resting tone is easier for the young musical mind than a similar melody that starts or ends on the third or even the fifth. The resting tone, as well as the progression to and from the resting tone, reinforces tonality in the musical mind. Songs with greater tonal challenges are appropriate only after children have developed the more advanced tonal skills of inferring and sustaining tonality without direct support from the song itself. Establishing tonality with the children prior to singing the song is helpful in securing tonality at all levels of development.

The purity of tonality in song is essential for the young musical mind. Alterations make tonality ambiguous. Modulations require greater skill. Shifting tonalities are much more difficult for the developing musical mind than shifting meters.

The difficulty of one tonality over another is not conclusive, but Dorian, Mixolydian, Phrygian, Lydian, and Aeolian focus the musical mind most immediately, with Phrygian sometimes seeming most compelling and Lydian most challenging. Songs in Lydian tonality have occasionally propelled an ensemble to a stunning choral sound not reached in other tonalities, as have songs in Phrygian. The tonal focus of the musical mind becomes manifest in tone quality, line, and ensemble sound as well as intonation. The purity of the less common tonalities so focus the musical mind that it leads one to wonder if perhaps Major and Minor tonalities might actually be the most difficult tonalities for the developing musical mind.

Assessing the tonal difficulty inherent in song guides us in choosing songs that are appropriate for our children's tonal development. It also helps us in rehearsal with any song literature. We often try to fix tonal issues through vocal technique. The inherent tonal difficulty might be the reason why children are singing out of tune, why singers struggle with pitches of a particular passage, or why they have trouble with what we might assume to be a simple entrance, interval, or accidental.

## Melody

Rhythm and tonal, each with their own inherent difficulty factors, come together as melody. Their intertwining influences the musical mind as it processes the two simultaneously, with or without text. Rhythm and tonal together can strengthen or complicate each other, supporting the musical mind or adding greater difficulty. Rhythm provides the foundation in the musical mind, with tonal on top, so underlying rhythm difficulty in song can confound tonal difficulty in the musical mind and affect the musical mind's processing of tonal.

Melody, with or without text, directs the attention of the musical mind to rhythm or to tonal. The musical mind is drawn to tonality, but rhythm can upstage tonal with its clever antics, distracting the musical mind from tonal and drawing attention to itself. The simpler the rhythm in songs both with and without words, the more the musical mind attends to tonal. The Aeolian melodies in Figure 3.12 and Figure 3.13 offer the same notes in the same order and in the same meter, but with different rhythm. The simplicity of rhythm in Figure 3.12, with its macro and micro beats, leads the musical mind to attend to tonal. The challenging rhythm of Figure 3.13 draws attention to itself, leading the musical mind to attend to rhythm more than tonal. Children will learn to handle tonal with more complex rhythms as they develop, but simple rhythms in song support tonality in the musical mind, developing the readiness for the musical mind to hold its own tonally amidst exciting rhythm.

**Figure 3.12**
Aeolian, simple rhythm

**Figure 3.13**
Aeolian, same pitches, difficult rhythm

The alignment in song between rhythm anchors (macro and micro beats) and tonal anchors (resting tone and fifth) support both a developing sense of meter and a developing sense of tonality, as the anticipated weight of both rhythm and tonal anchors reinforce each other. Macro beats in Figure 3.14 in Minor tonality fall primarily on the resting tone and fifth, supporting both meter and tonality in the musical mind. The anticipated resting tone in the descending passage coincides with the anticipated weight of macro beats, further supporting both meter and tonality in the musical mind. The developing musical mind thrives when rhythm and tonal work together to support it.

**Figure 3.14**
Minor, with alignment between rhythm and tonal anchors

A lack of synchrony between the weight of macro and micro beats and the implied weight of resting tone and fifth demands more of the musical mind, forcing it to maintain metric or tonal anchors amidst the distraction of unpredictable weight distribution, without support for those anchors in sound. The challenge of a lack of alignment between rhythm and tonal is akin to syncopation, within which the weight of the melodic rhythm does not align with the anticipated weight of macro and micro beats, requiring the musical mind to work harder to maintain the meter. Figure 3.15, in contrast to Figure 3.14, presents the same pitches in the same order as Figure 3.14, but in Triple meter, demonstrating less alignment between rhythm and tonal. Meter and tonality would be far more secure in the musical mind with the melody in Figure 3.14 than with that of Figure 3.15.

**Figure 3.15**
Minor, with less alignment between rhythm and tonal anchors

The weight of meter can also support a developing sense of tonality by its alignment with characteristic tones, reinforcing the uniqueness of the tonality. Macro beats in the Mixolydian melody in Figure 3.16 frequently fall on the characteristic seventh as well as on the resting tone and fifth. Melodic contour can support a developing sense of meter, with its line, twists, turns, climax, or repose aligning with the weight of meter. Each of these occurrences might suggest harmonic alignment as well, with the weight of meter aligning with the anticipated weight of harmonic functions that define the tonality. Harmonic alignment can surely support both a sense of meter and a sense of tonality, but the musical mind needs the transparency of rhythm and tonal in the unison melodic line, accompanied only by movement, to learn to navigate musicality. (See Appendix D for harmonic functions that define the various tonalities.)

**Figure 3.16**
Mixolydian, alignment also with characteristic seventh

Songs that support the musical mind's developing sense of meter and developing sense of tonality, wherever the children are in that process, propel children's artistry and develop the readiness for songs of greater difficulty. A song with challenging rhythm will not teach the underlying rhythm skills necessary to navigate difficult rhythm with tonal, nor the underlying tonal skills necessary to navigate tonality amidst difficult rhythm. Children can, of course, learn to sing a song the musical mind doesn't have the readiness for, just as they can learn to recite a poem in a language they do not understand. The experience, however, will not develop the musical understanding that would transfer to more difficult choral literature; and performance will be compromised without the musical mind's command in sound of the meter, tonality, and musical complexity.

Children's musical readiness for a song is dependent upon the rhythm and tonal development of the musical mind. Rhythm readiness includes a developing sense of meter, some competence in the meter of the song, and some familiarity with melodic rhythm patterns in that meter that are on the difficulty level of those of the song. Tonal readiness includes a developing sense of tonality, some competence with the tonality of the song, plus rhythm readiness for the melodic rhythm, since tonal is a layer on top of rhythm.

The musical mind in song works like a tower of blocks. Rhythm provides the foundation, with macro beats underlying micro beats and the more difficult melodic rhythm on top, dependent upon the solidity of macro and micro beats for its security. The tonal dimension adds another layer of difficulty on top of melodic rhythm, with a solid structure of rhythm blocks necessary to keep the stack of blocks balanced. Text is yet another layer on top of rhythm and melody, with instrumental accompaniments and vocal parts adding still more layers. Any individual layer that is not secure in the musical mind can topple the entire structure. The stability of rhythm and tonal blocks at every level of difficulty is essential to create a sound structure that can support text, accompaniment, and parts.

Songs of ongoing difficulty that match the rhythm and tonal developmental of children support the musical mind at every level. They help the musical mind to sustain its rhythm development and tonal development, now in the context of rhythm, melody, and text. They challenge the musical mind to embody the occasional rhythmic figure or melodic contour not previously encountered. They enable children to apply rhythm and tonal development in the acquisition of artistic expression and vocal technique.

## Text

Song texts that promote children's artistry reflect the magnificence of children. They resonate with something deep within children that may or may not align with the thinking mind. They inspire the poetry that is children. They touch the love, joy, and sensitivity that children embody at every age, drawing out feelingful expression from within. Songs that give voice to children's artistry are musical translations of such texts.

What the text is about is not what text is about in relation to children's artistry. The text of a song that serves developing artistry is the script of a play of musical energy, in which melody and rhythm create the musical equivalent of staging, scenery, characters, costumes, and expression of the script. Every musical dimension is in service of the words, which come with their own rhythm, melody, expression, sound, and energy. The rhythm and spirit of the words are reflected in the melodic rhythm, tempo, and momentum of the song. The spoken expression of the text is reflected in the melodic direction, intensity of the line, twists, turns, and peak of phrase. The sound and meaning of the words are reflected in the mood, style, and intensity of the musical setting.

Difficulty factors of text include the sophistication of the words, their imagery, meaning, and emotional import; the combination of words, their sound and ease in pronunciation; text length, repetition, number of verses, and language; but the musical setting of text is the greater determinant of song difficulty, whatever the difficulty of text. The way the text intertwines with rhythm and melody can compound the difficulty of rhythm, melody, and text, individually and together. Songs that most serve children's artistry articulate the most natural expression of the words of any text, both rhythmically and melodically. Rhythm and melodic anchors, aligned in support of the musical mind, further align with syllabic and emphatic delivery of text, supporting the natural expression of text.

Delivery of the translated haiku text in Figure 3.17, set in Unusual Paired meter and Dorian tonality, aligns with the give-and-take of the meter, and with the twists and turns of the melodic contour. Meter, tonality, and the expression of text support each other. Figure 3.18, on the other hand, presents the same text and the same pitches in the same order, with the same duration in the easier Duple meter, demonstrating a lack of alignment between text, melody, and rhythm. The second example does not support meter and tonality in the musical mind, nor the natural expression of the words, making it more difficult for children than the setting in Unusual Paired meter.

**Figure 3.17**
Dorian, Unusual Paired

# A Pair of Butterflies

**Figure 3.18**
Dorian, Duple

The all-important setting of text also determines the quality of a song. A simple text set beautifully, particularly in one of the less common tonalities, can yield fine art. A trite text can become highly musical in a fine playful setting, tickling the musical mind's sense of humor. The quality of a song with a beautiful text is only as good as the musical realization of that text.

Songs that serve children's artistry offer texts appropriate to the expressive range of the children, as well as settings appropriate to the children's music development. Five- and six-year-old children with extensive experience in meters and tonalities can have the musical readiness for songs of greater musical sophistication than their age might lead us to believe, but they need texts that match their innocence. Ten- and eleven-year-old beginners, on the other hand, need song texts that respect their older maturity, yet with rhythm and melody that match their beginning musicality.

Children's artistry most reveals itself in songs that meet the musical needs of children, with texts that resonate with the essence of childhood, settings that put into music what language puts into words, and emotional import that is within grasp of the age. Songs that meet these criteria mobilize the life force of children of all ages and stages. They unveil the wonder of the child, the wonder of the musical mind, and the wonder of children's artistry at every level.

# Dance To Your Daddie

**Figure 3.19**
Mixolydian, Triple

*Dance to Your Daddie* (Figure 3.19), the Scottish rhyme set in Mixolydian tonality and Triple meter, offers an example of a simple text for young children with a more sophisticated musical setting. The song is appropriate for five- and six-year-old children with some musical maturity developed through experience in the various meters and tonalities. Let's take a look at this song in relation to the establishment of meter and tonality, the inherent difficulty presented in rhythm, tonal challenges, and alignment between rhythm, tonal, and text.

The rhythm both supports and challenges the young musical mind. The song establishes Triple meter in the first measure, though with the inclusion of divisions, requires greater skill in Triple meter than a song establishing meter more simply with just macro and micro beats. The dotted rhythms add to rhythm difficulty, as do ties. The tied notes, being tied to macro beats, make the rhythmic figures after each of these ties function as upbeat patterns, increasing rhythm difficulty still more.

There is quite a contrast in feel between the lilting dance statement with its tie and repeat, and the more weighty "fishy" section, reflecting the rhythm of the rhyme. The natural expression of the text, created rhythmically with the tie in the 6/8 section, creates the feel of only one macro beat in each measure, with triple divisions of two micro beats. The contrast in weight to the single macro beat in each measure of the 3/8 section makes it feel as if macro beats of the two sections are in two different tempos. The subtlety supports children's artistic expression of the text, while engaging them in musicality beyond what might typically be expected of such young children.

The melody establishes Mixolydian tonality in the first measure, even without the sixth, supporting the developing sense of tonality, and fully distinguishing Mixolydian tonality from Major with the continued recurrence of Mixolydian's characteristic seventh. The opening of the song on the fifth rather than the resting tone adds to tonal difficulty. The melody hovers around and between the resting tone and fifth, with the melodic contour that draws the musical mind to tonality. It offers the ease of abundant stepwise passages and skips between the resting tone and fifth, yet offers a bit more challenge with skips within the harmonic functions that define the tonality.

Macro beats align with the resting tone and fifth, or with the characteristic seventh of Mixolydian, reinforcing tonality and meter in the musical mind. Rhythm and melodic anchors align with the recited pronunciation and energy of the words. The musical sophistication of the setting compels the musical mind and propels artistry, though with a simple text. The addition of a piano accompaniment, with an interlude between repetitions of the song, makes *Dance to Your Daddie* suitable for concert with kindergarten and first graders. Young singers ready for the musical challenges perform songs like this with the musicality and poise of choral musicians, deserving to sing the songs twice through in concert. (Piano accompaniments for songs presented in this chapter can be found in the Come Children Sing Institute SONG LIBRARY at www.comechildrensing.com/sl.php.)

## Artistic Expression

Songs that give voice to children's artistry evoke artistic expression. Their rhythm and melody mirror the drama of the words, illuminate the text, and compel the musical mind, making the song and its expression irresistible for children. The song, itself, becomes like the parent reading a bedtime story with vocal inflection and intensity depicting characters and dramatizing storyline, drawing the child into the middle of the narrative through evocative delivery, and demonstrating how to be expressive in the narrative.

The melody makes the text come alive, and the text makes the melody come alive. Melody serves as teacher for the expression of the text, supporting every vocal inflexion of the spoken text through the musical setting. The text serves as coach for the expression of the musical line, supporting every musical nuance through the natural expression of text and its resonance with children. Teacher and coach together take children on a journey into the choral art, demonstrating how to be expressive in song and inspiring heartfelt performance from children of all ages. Singing children literally become the song, with the kind of passion and deliberateness that characterize quality performance at all levels of choral artistry.

Children who throughout elementary school sing quality songs of increasing difficulty that meet their musical needs, with well-set texts that resonate with childhood, regularly sing musical lines that build, rhythms that twist and turn, and musical settings that trace the drama of text. They experience in an ongoing manner what it feels like to be expressive in songs of different styles, tempos, texts, and difficulty, developing both the model and readiness for the kind of expressive singing we aspire to achieve with more advanced choral literature.

Children with extensive experience with songs whose musical settings support the meaningful delivery of text apply that experience to songs of greater musical complexity when the melodic line may not guide heartfelt delivery of text so directly. Children with extensive experience with songs whose texts support the musical building of lines, articulation of phrases, and expression of musical nuance apply that experience to songs with more challenging texts that may not guide musical delivery so directly.

Songs that meet the musical needs of children, with beautifully set, heartfelt texts, tap into the breadth of children's expression in addition to the riches of the musical mind, providing the vehicle of song for their joyous, tandem release. They scaffold children's expressive delivery, just as they do their developing sense of meter and sense of tonality, supporting fledgling choral artistry musically and expressively at every level.

Children's experience of the wonder of their own artistry in song motivates every age to engage in the choral art. It feeds musicality with instrumental music. It can foster a lifetime of making exciting music.

# Where Are My Roses?

**Figure 3.20**
Aeolian, Triple

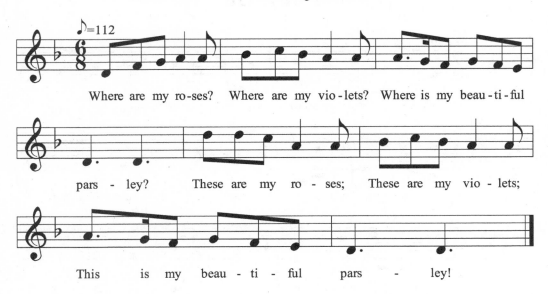

*Where Are My Roses?* (Figure 3.20), with text from ancient Greece, draws children right into the choral art and into their own capacity for artistry. Song architecture helps us to better understand why this song of such brevity and simplicity can draw such expressive delivery from children, despite the seeming irrelevance of "beautiful parsley."

Aeolian tonality and Triple meter assure the engagement of the awakened musical mind. Both meter and tonality are defined within the first two measures, securing children's developing sense of meter and sense of tonality. The relatively simple rhythm, though in Triple meter and more difficult than just macro and micro beats, directs the focus of the musical mind to tonality, leading the musical mind toward tone and shape of line, as well as intonation. The melody spins around the resting tone and fifth, with abundant stepwise passages, starting and ending on the resting tone. The weight of macro beats regularly aligns with the implied weight of resting tone and fifth, further supporting the musical mind.

The text is within the grasp of five- and six-year-old children, as is its musical setting. Rhythm and melody mirror the natural expression of the words. Rhythm and tonal anchors align with the syllabic delivery of text. The shape of the melody reflects the emotional expression of the spoken word text, with greater intensity in the triumph of finding what has been lost, and then bringing the text to resolution. The melodic rhythm and melodic contour both support the expression of text and the emotional import of the song, as well as supporting the musical mind.

Introducing this song through several repetitions that grow out of Aeolian tonality narrative in Triple meter transports children directly into the choral art, where they receive the words as poets and express their own beauty through such innocent, child-like expression. Musical movement propels expressive delivery, making all dimensions of artistry more tangible. This little song can serve to bring the music class or chorus into the choral art. It can serve as a choral warm-up with older singers. The addition of a piano accompaniment, with an interlude between repetitions, makes the song a lovely performance piece with kindergarten and first graders.

**Figure 3.21**
Mixolydian, Multimetric—
Unusual Unpaired/Duple

# Penguin

*Penguin* (Figure 3.21) offers a very different kind of song, text, and expression for children with greater music development. Its challenging rhythm in Mixolydian tonality upstages tonal, directing the focus of the musical mind to rhythm. The shifting meters are well within the realm of kindergarten and first graders with a strong foundation in meter, though sixth grade beginners would not yet have the musical readiness for this song.

The whimsical text could serve a broad range of ages. The rhythm and tempo of the song reflect the natural expression of the sprightly text, while the shifting meters capture the child's spontaneous and enthusiastic delivery of such delight. The melody, with its ups and downs, steps, multiple skips within the harmonic functions that define the tonality, and difficult rhythm, mirror the child's playful expression of the text, while offering greater melodic challenge than *Where Are My Roses?* Rhythm and tonal anchors align with each other and with syllabic pronunciation of text.

Rhythm challenge demands a fairly well-developed sense of meter, with sufficient tonal security to sustain Mixolydian tonality amidst such challenging rhythm. *Penguin* serves well in the music classroom or chorus with a variety of ages, or as a warm-up with older singers, accompanied only by musical movement. The addition of piano accompaniment with interlude between repetitions makes *Penguin* a delightful piece for concert.

The contrast between *Where Are My Roses?* and *Penguin* is evident. One focuses the musical mind on tonal, the other on rhythm. The two songs differ in style, text, tempo, type of expression, and musical difficulty, yet the text of each can serve five- and six-year-old children, with *Penguin* appropriate for older children as well. The two songs meet the musical needs of children of different levels of music development.

Take another look now at *Dance to Your Daddie* compared to *Where Are My Roses?* and *Penguin*. The expression of each text is supported by its musical translation. Where do you feel that *Dance to Your Daddie* fits with the other two in terms of musical and expressive demands? How do you view rhythm difficulty of the three songs in relation to each other? How do you view relative tonal difficulty of the three songs? How do you view the expressive challenges of each piece in relation to the others? *Dance to Your Daddie's* musically sophisticated rhythm and melodic contour requires greater rhythm and tonal readiness than *Where Are My Roses?,* yet not as much as *Penguin*, with its shifting meters and demand for tonal security amidst exciting rhythm.

## Vocal Technique

Songs that give voice to children's artistry cultivate vocal technique. They capture the musical mind, which commands the vocal instrument. They ignite artistic expression, which empowers the vocal instrument. They elicit the optimal sound of children's voices, which enables the vocal instrument.

The architecture of songs that give voice to children's artistry supports the vocal instrument just as it supports the musical mind and artistic expression. Head voice is prompted and sustained by vocal placement and melodic contour. Breath and energy are charged by expression of appropriate text mirrored in rhythm and melody. Line and tone come alive through tonality, melodic contour, the energy of the line, and the melodic translation of text. Articulation is fostered by secure meter and the rhythmic and melodic translation of text. Intonation, momentum, and rhythmic precision are secured through support of the musical mind. The vocal, musical, and expressive dimensions of songs that give voice to children's artistry lead children at every level to experience the vocal technique needed to sing the songs beautifully.

Vocal technique, often coached from the outside, emerges from the inside through the development of the musical mind, the use of musical movement, and songs that give voice to children's artistry. The musical mind guides the vocal instrument as it learns to navigate musicality and vocal range. Heartfelt expression incites embodied expression, motivating breath and sustaining a supported tone through the artistic delivery of line. Musical movement propels musicality, energy, and expressivity. There may occasionally be a need to prompt vocal technique, but when the songs themselves and musical movement generate appropriate vocal technique, there is far less need for such prompting. Vocal technique grows in the context of musicality and its natural expression through the musical mind and body.

Children's execution of each song provides experience with and a model for the kind of musicality, expression, and choral sound we strive to achieve with more difficult literature. Songs that stir the souls of children lead to expressive singing that becomes exemplary for all song literature. Songs with optimal vocal placement that focus the musical mind tonally lead to a quality sound that becomes a model for other choral literature. Songs that focus the musical mind rhythmically lead to vitality and deliberate execution to emulate with any repertoire. Children who experience the ongoing difficulty of songs that give voice to children's artistry throughout childhood develop the readiness musically, expressively, and vocally at every step to engage in songs that require greater musicality, greater expressivity, and greater vocal technique.

Children with a secure musical mind move competently from the singing range that best serves the musical mind to the singing range that best serves the vocal instrument. The musical mind and its expression develop most in the range from middle C to the B♭ above, with a tessitura between D and A, whereas the child voice really resonates above that range. The initial singing range is where the musical mind makes the most sense of tonal—a sense of tonality. It is the range in which the musical mind learns to speak—to deliver tonal knowing through the voice. This beginning singing range serves for immersion and interaction with tonal narratives in the various tonalities with singers of all ages. This range offers the most immediate access to the musical mind—our portal for capturing the musical mind tonally, keeping it at the forefront, and taking it into the choral art, without the encumbrance of the thinking mind or vocal technique.

Songs that give voice to children's artistry move children effortlessly into the higher range, compelling the musical mind to guide pitch, intonation, and vocal quality. They mobilize the expression of the child, generating breath and support for the higher range. Children with extensive experience in the various tonalities in the initial singing range quite naturally navigate the voice break around the B above middle C ($C_4$), singing in tune, without any prompting of head voice. This smooth transition through the voice break up to $D_5$, a ninth above middle C, assures a quality sound above the voice break, where the child voice rings. Songs in the range from middle C to $G_5$ a 12th above, with a tessitura between $E_4$ and $E_5$ elicit the quality sound that we hear in fine children's choruses and can elicit in every music classroom.

*Where Are My Roses?* (Figure 3.20) moves children gently beyond the voice break, supporting vocal technique through the gradual rise and fall of the expressive melodic line with abundant stepwise passages and secure tonality. The drama of the text reflected in the octave leap and melodic contour stimulates breath for the higher range and brings that supported breath into the expression of the rest of the line.

The tessitura of *Dance to Your Daddie* (Figure 3.19) is a bit higher, though also going only to the D above the voice break. This song stimulates greater vocal technique than *Where Are My Roses?* with its placement around the voice break, its opening in the higher range requiring greater breath support, and the melodic windup to the second measure leading to the repeat with its need for breath support. Children who can sing songs like *Where Are My Roses?* and *Dance to Your Daddie* beautifully are ready to move the voice higher.

*Penguin* (Figure 3.21) takes the voice up to an E♭, with much of the melody in that higher range, requiring and stimulating still greater vocal technique than either of the other two songs, in addition to requiring greater rhythm and tonal development. The musicality, expressive import, and tessitura of each song enable vocal technique in children that are musically ready for these songs.

# Autumn Thought

**Figure 3.22**
Minor, Triple

*Autumn Thought* (Figure 3.22), with the lovely text of Langston Hughes, places children's voices in the optimal range, with heightened emphasis above the voice break, supporting sound in that range through musical and expressive dimensions. The setting in Minor tonality and Triple meter focuses the musical mind, with the opening figure securing meter and tempo. The natural expression of the words presents greater rhythmic challenge than the simpler *Where Are My Roses?* with the many divisions of micro beats, long notes, and the jagged "happy," "summer," and "withered." The text itself is more difficult than *Where Are My Roses?*

The melody defines Minor tonality, and spins around and between the resting tone and fifth with greater freedom than the easier *Where Are My Roses?* It includes abundant stepwise passages but offers greater challenge with its starting on the fifth rather than the resting tone, its skip of a sixth, and sustained pitches, demanding more from the singer musically and vocally. Rhythm anchors are in alignment with tonal anchors or characteristic tones, and with word pronunciation.

Langston Hughes' words offer a childlike expression of the wonder of nature that is within the grasp of children from kindergarten on up. The natural expression of the words presents the first statement somewhat casually, and then builds the drama with the skip and higher placement of the second phrase, reaching the peak of the song in the third phrase with considerable intensity, and then gently resolving into a graceful dance. This song supports children's dramatic delivery of the text, scaffolding expression through the energy of the line. It also supports vocal technique, as the drama of the second phrase as well as its pitch level demands greater breath support than the first, with the long note increasing intensity to the peak of the song, which requires still greater breath support. The contrast between the line building to the peak of the song and the graceful dance invites children to be artists.

This song mobilizes children's artistry, with musicality as the driving force. Children capture every musical nuance of this song through singing and movement. Musical movement reflects and reinforces the expression of line and the contrast of the dance, while also moving energy into breath and vocal production. Children find excitement in their own artistry as they reach the peak of the song, hearing and feeling the expressive power of their own voices in creating the drama of the song. Children deserve to sing the song in concert, with piano accompaniment and interlude between repetitions of the song.

**Figure 3.23**
Phrygian, Triple

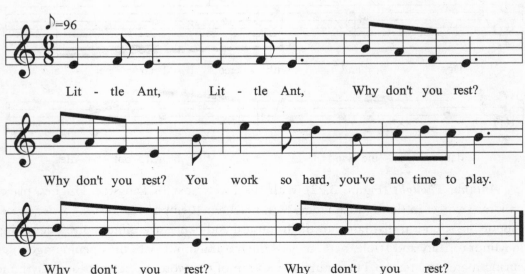

# Ant

*Ant* (Figure 3.23) draws a beautiful sound out of children, eliciting pure child expression and the thrill of heartfelt singing shaping a quality sound. The reflective text, set in the optimal range in Phrygian tonality and Triple meter, generates a highly musical experience, leading children's voices to ring. Rhythm defines the meter and tempo, but the opening figure requires a bit more skill with Triple meter than the three micro beat opening in both *Autumn Thought* and *Where Are My Roses?*

The melody clearly secures Phrygian tonality from the start, as the somewhat haunting, repeated opening figure with the lowered second presents the most characteristic sound of Phrygian. The melody spins around the resting tone and fifth, with stepwise passages and skips drawing the musical mind to tonality through its contour. Macro and micro beats align with resting tone and fifth or characteristic tones, reinforcing both tonality and meter in the musical mind. They also align with text pronunciation, facilitating musical delivery. The song increases in intensity throughout, with the first two measures contemplative, the next two with the greater intensity of pitch and deliberate questioning, and the peak of the song expressing compassion for the ant with the strength of children's passion, breath energy, and vocal sound.

The song leads the musical mind with the readiness for *Ant* to greater focus on tonal, with its simple rhythm, directing the musical mind's attention to vocal sound and stimulating a quality sound without instruction about head voice. The shape of the line and expression of text bring the head voice from the top of the range down into the lower range, encouraging consistency in sound quality throughout the range. The shape and energy of the line with its building intensity further promotes quality sound. Children who are producing a lovely sound in *Ant* are excited to create a still more beautiful sound by minimizing the diphthong in the word "why," shading the vowel to an "ah," and diminishing the "r" in the words "work" and "hard" and the "n" in the word "ant." Children love shaping sound as choral artists.

This song scaffolds the musical mind, children's expression, and vocal technique. Its rhythm and melody offer the vehicle for full-hearted expression, releasing the life force of children with their inquiring reverence for nature's creatures. The song inspires children's artistry in all dimensions, leading to artistic expression, vocal support, and quality sound.

Movement enhances the learning and delivery of this song, reflecting the growing intensity, energizing breath for the peak of the song in the heat of the drama, maintaining Triple meter, and expressing the passion children feel with this song. *Ant* can serve in the primary grade classroom or as a warm-up with older singers. The addition of a piano accompaniment, with an interlude between repetitions, provides for a lovely concert presentation. *Ant* was written for musically developed kindergarten and first graders, but has been used with many ages, including college singers. A song for children that draws artistry, like a beautiful children's poem, knows no age.

**Weasel** (Figure 3.24) presents a complete contrast to *Ant*, though both are in Phrygian tonality. *Weasel* invites a very different kind of expression from children, one just as passionate as that evoked by *Ant*, but highlighting a very different side of children. *Weasel*, unlike *Ant*, does not focus the musical mind directly on sound, but rather on the fast and furious articulation of rhythm and tongue-twisting text that expresses the delightful nature of the child. The setting in Duple meter and its quick tempo match the expression of text. The rhythm, with its starting pick-up notes, rests, and elongated

**Figure 3.24**
Phrygian, Duple

48

# Weasel

I saw a wea-sel, a wea-sel, A

long and slen-der, small and fur-ry, Light-ning quick and

full of fur-y, Wea-sel, a

wea-sel. I know I saw a

wea-sel, wea-sel, wea-sel. It

could have been a squir-rel, But I know it was a

wea-sel. A wea-sel, a

wea-sel, A long and slen-der, small and fur-ry,

**Figure 3.24**
Continued

49

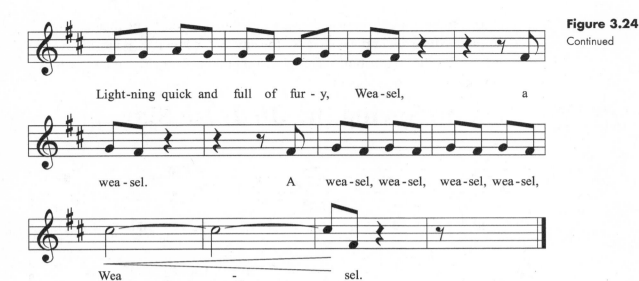

ending increase the difficulty of Duple meter. Security in Duple meter will assure that the tongue-twister text will fall in place, as well as the rhythmic challenges.

The melody clearly defines Phrygian tonality, with reinforcement of the characteristic lowered second, and contour around and between the resting tone and fifth. The setting places children in the optimal vocal range, with a lot of stepwise passages and jumps between tonic and dominant. Rhythm anchors are aligned with resting tone, fifth, or characteristic tones, as well as with text. The quick tempo in the higher range and the long pitch at the end of the song stimulate vocal technique to match the challenge, but the greater challenge of this song is in its rhythm, text articulation, and tempo, and in maintaining Phrygian tonality amidst such exciting rhythm. Singing a song like *Ant* beautifully, with its focus on tone, helps to prepare the musical mind to sustain tonality in a song like *Weasel*, with its driving rhythm.

The expression of *Weasel* captures children's excitement in reporting and making a big deal of their experience, throwing off the slightest doubt, and delivering their story with passion. The rhythm and melody support that kind of expression through the shape, direction, and energy of the line, the tempo, and setting of text. The crescendo at the end of the song is as natural an expression for children in the context of their telling their story as it is in the context of the song. Children with the musical readiness for this song cannot help but sing *Weasel* with energy, passion, and deliberateness, the very qualities we long to achieve in more advanced choral literature.

Movement, with weighted macro beats in the meter, helps to secure tempo within the meter, pumping energy into vocal technique and expression of the final pronouncement. Add a piano accompaniment with an interlude between repetitions of *Weasel*, and you have a song for all ages that is electric in performance.

Songs like *Ant* and *Where Are My Roses?*, with their focus on tonal, can do wonders to develop sound, whereas songs like *Weasel* and *Penguin*, with their more compelling and intricate rhythmic structures, propel vitality, momentum, and articulation. Songs like

*Autumn Thought* present a nice balance between rhythm and tonal, encouraging sound, momentum, and expression in the context of tonality and meter. The sound achieved in a song like *Ant*, and the articulation achieved in a song like *Weasel* become models that can be brought into any song literature.

**Figure 3.25**
Lydian, Duple

# In Spring the Birds Do Sing

*In Spring the Birds Do Sing* (Figure 3.25), an effective warm–up in Lydian tonality and Duple meter, offers the voice practice in navigating the voice break with agility, while maintaining vocal quality through each of the slurs and sustaining Lydian tonality. Starting the second pitch of each slur with an aspirated "H" eases the challenge of delivering the second pitch with the same precision as the first until the children can execute the slurs without the "H." The setting of the English rhyme hovers around the voice break, highlighting the raised fourth, the characteristic tone of Lydian that distinguishes it from Major tonality.

This song establishes and maintains meter and tonality. Melodic contour, a bit of rhythmic challenge, and alignment between rhythm, melody, and text support the musical mind. Children who sing the final descending passage with a flat fourth are demonstrating that they are processing the song in Major tonality rather than Lydian, and that they need considerably more experience in the various tonalities to be able to deliver Lydian precisely. This song has been used as a warm–up with college singers, both for the musical mind and for vocal technique, and it has been used in a demonstration concert with elementary grade singers, with a solo demo from a volunteer first grader sung beautifully in tune.

*Oh Star* (Figure 3.26), with its setting in Minor tonality and Triple meter, demands and stimulates greater vocal technique. Song architecture and expression lead children to support the voice in the higher range, and to bring that sound quality back into the lower register. Children who are attuned to tonality and meter, who have the experience of singing songs like *Where Are My Roses?*, *Autumn Thought*, and *Ant* beautifully, have the readiness for the artistic challenges of *Oh Star*. Ensemble sound takes flight in this song, as does children's artistry.

# Oh Star

**Figure 3.26**
Minor, Triple

51

The song, itself, invites artistry. It establishes tonality and meter, with some rhythmic challenge as well as increased range. Rhythm anchors align with resting tone, fifth, characteristic tones, and text pronunciation. The melody spins around and between tonal anchors and includes abundant stepwise passages. Range and tessitura stimulate quality sound. Song rhythm expresses text in its simplicity, rather than drawing attention to itself, focusing greater attention to tonality and sound. The text lends itself to creating a beautiful sound, as the words "star," "shine," "bright," "all," and "night" can be shaded to the open "ah" sound, minimizing the distortion of the "r," "n," and "l," and opening the voice throughout. The text is within the emotional range of children who are ready for the musical and vocal challenges.

The melodic contour of *Oh Star*—the initial statement in the lower range, building with the second phrase to the peak of the third phrase, and then resolving back down to the resting tone—is one of the most powerful song contours for children. It draws the heart and soul out of children, with impassioned vocal sound and expression that embodies artistry. Children thrill in creating such artistic expression, bringing the sound quality of the higher range into the lower range because it is beautiful expression, and because the melodic contour of the song, reflecting the drama of the text, inspires the sensitivity and necessary vocal technique to do so. Children's stunning performance of this song, with the addition of a piano accompaniment with interlude between repetitions, shines like a star in any concert.

*Oh Star* directs the musical mind to sound and expression more than to rhythm. Rehearsal with weighted macro and micro beat movement in Triple meter helps to secure the momentum of meter. *Oh Star* was presented to over 200 choral conductors at a national convention of the American Choral Directors' Association. The sound from so many choral musicians was stunning, but it wasn't until weighted macro and micro beat movement was employed underneath that beautiful sound that *Oh Star* was delivered by the ensemble of professional musicians with true artistry.

## Advancing Artistry

Unison songs of increasing difficulty that scaffold the musical mind, artistic expression, and vocal technique provide for children's ongoing growth musically, expressively, and vocally, both individually and in ensemble. The purity of the single line offers children the most intimate experience with the choral art, with their own artistry, and with a community of singers.

Children encounter greater musical complexity through the increasing difficulty of rhythm, tonal, text, and their interplay. Every new challenge kindles the energy of the line of unison song. Every musical nuance is a push and pull of that energy, propelling children musically, expressively, and vocally at every level, with each unison song taking children deeper into the choral art.

A song that cannot stand on its own musicality, without instrumental accompaniment or vocal parts, is not worthy of children's artistry. A piano accompaniment offers a meaningful dimension for performance, but only after children can sing the unison song beautifully. Choral parts that support the musical mind, artistic expression, and vocal technique are appropriate only after children can beautifully sing unison songs of considerable musical sophistication. Children need a lot of direct experience with the art, navigating musicality in the unison line to develop the readiness for choral parts, and to develop the readiness for notation to become the mediator between song and artistry. Unison songs of increasing difficulty that give voice to children's artistry offer individuals and the ensemble the ongoing musical complexity regularly encountered in vocal and instrumental solo repertoire, without the encumbrance of choral parts or notation, developing artistry that can then be brought to those dimensions.

Ensemble sound soars in unison songs that give voice to children's artistry, accompanied only by movement. The experience of singing beautifully in ensemble becomes its own motivation. The community of artists becomes one in sound, one in expression, and one in the thrill of making exciting music together.

*Starfish* (Figure 3.27) offers rhythmic complexity with a heartfelt text, reflecting children's marvel of nature through melodic line, shifting meters, and ponderous tempo with rubato-like feel. This song requires development of the musical mind to secure and sustain shifting meters, with its various combinations of threes and twos in both meter and rhythm. The rhythm presents children's natural expression of the questions of the text, including the slow tempo and give and take of the feel of rubato. Children with the musical maturity for *Starfish* find greater ease with the rhythmic challenges than might a teacher reading the notation.

The song establishes Aeolian tonality, but with the slightest ambiguity. It offers abundant stepwise passages but presents tonal challenge. The opening and successive questions all start on the third. The anchor of the fifth appears only late in the song, requiring more of the musical mind, which is supported by the alignment of rhythm, tonal, and text. The melodic contour captures children's curiosity about the starfish with growing intensity to the peak of the song, generating artistic expression, breath support and energy. Vocal placement encourages vocal maturity, as does the challenge of maintaining a beautiful sound amidst the song's rhythmic complexity. The repeated "Starfish," with the elongated second syllable at the beginning of each of the first three lines creates a challenge rhythmically, expressively, and vocally. Minimizing the "r" in "Starfish," coloring the short "i" sound with a bit of the brighter "ee" sound, placing the "sh" at the end

# Starfish

**Figure 3.27**
Aeolian, Multimetric—
Triple/Duple

53

of the long notes, and minimizing the "w" in "how" make the lovely sound inspired by this song even more beautiful. The shape of the melody culminating in the dramatic climax that resolves back down to the resting tone is the shape that draws the heart and soul of children expressively and vocally. Children become as lost in their own artistry with this song as they do in the wonder of the starfish.

Children who have artfully executed songs like *Oh Star* are ready for *Starfish* and for the give and take of the energy of the line, preparing them for such musical challenges in more advanced choral literature. Beautiful singing and a piano accompaniment with an interlude between repetitions make *Starfish* concert-ready.

***African Dance*** (Figure 3.28), with the descriptive words of Langston Hughes set in Aeolian tonality and shifting meters, offers yet another kind of expression. The ongoing "beating of the tom toms," literally reflected on a continuing resting tone, create a kind of consistency, yet tension throughout. The shifting meters add to the drama yet feel very natural in the expression of the text. Tonal is not as challenging as the rhythm of this song, supporting the musical mind with its constant return to the resting tone, abundant stepwise passages, and skips between resting tone and fifth. The alignment of rhythm, tonal, and text encourage musical delivery. Tonality, vocal placement, melodic contour, and expressive import stimulate a supported sound, with the challenge of maintaining that sound amidst the complex rhythm.

*African Dance* requires maturity musically, expressively, and vocally. The dance of the girl who "whirls" in rhythm and pitch in a "circle of light" is unpredictable, yet natural, just as the dance suggested by the words. Children's artistry dances with the girl, creating

**54**

**Figure 3.28**
Aeolian, Multimetric—
Unusual Paired/Duple/
Unusual Unpaired/Triple

# African Dance

a graceful, fluid, and compelling dance, with a smooth transition back and forth from the beating of the tom toms. Shifting meters and melodic contour create the energy in the dance needed to deliver the poem expressively and with appropriate vocal technique. Children's expression of this song can "stir your blood," as the poem suggests. A piano accompaniment rounds out the presentation for performance.

# May Night

**Figure 3.29**
Dorian, Duple

55

♪=90

The spring is fresh and fear - less And eve - ry leaf is new, The world is brimmed with moon - light, The li - lac brimmed with dew. Here in the mov - ing shad - ows I catch my breath and sing-- My heart is fresh and fear - less and o - ver brimmed with spring.

*May Night* (Figure 3.29), with the lovely words of Sara Teasdale presented in Dorian tonality and Duple meter, invites the child to become one with the beauty of the unfolding spring. The musical narrative, melodically, rhythmically, and textually, paints the picture, with the excitement in the energy of the line leading the child to his own artistry.

*May Night* presents some difficulty, yet the rhythm, which reflects the natural expression of the words, is simple compared to *African Dance*. Tonal, also, is not complex, with its abundant stepwise passages, its spinning around and to and from the resting tone and fifth, and its alignment with rhythm and text. The song establishes and sustains meter and tonality.

The text requires some maturity but is appropriate for children with the readiness for the musical and vocal challenges. This song stretches children most in relation to vocal technique, with vocal placement generally above the voice break, the anticipatory tension in the expression of the line, and peak of the song on the high F needing substantial support. The melodic line, reflecting the drama of the text, captures the excitement of a breathtaking spring, while stimulating the breath needed in the delivery of the drama. Children demonstrate uncommon artistry in this song. A piano accompaniment and interlude between repetitions of *May Night* give the audience and the children the joy of savoring such artistry with the repetition in concert.

**Figure 3.30**
Mixolydian, Multimetric—
Unusual Unpaired/
Triple/Duple

# The Bird's Carol

**Figure 3.30**
Continued

57

*The Bird's Carol* (Figure 3.30), set in Mixolydian tonality and shifting meters, offers children the opportunity to exercise their playful and highly musical selves. Children with competence in meter and tonality handle the shifting meters with ease, and effortlessly sing the compelling caroling section with fine intonation and breath support. The quick tempo through the varying meters showcases children's delight in being so musical.

The shifting meters in sound and movement are very natural with the text and the melody, despite the melodic line that is more angular than *May Night*. Vocal placement highlights the sound of children's voices, while the energy of the line draws children into artistic expression, empowering vocal technique to deliver skillfully. The *Bird's Carol* demands significant musical maturity, rhythmically, tonally, expressively, and vocally, while scaffolding every one of those dimensions. A piano accompaniment that supports the meter, tonality, energy of the line, and playfulness of the song adds to a polished performance of the joyous carol.

Piano accompaniments that serve children's artistry, like the songs, clearly define meter and tonality, supporting both throughout the song without ambiguity, without accidentals, and without rhythm flourish that distracts the musical mind. Harmonic structures or implications are those that define the tonality; and rhythm, tonal, and harmonic anchors align with those of the song. Appropriate accompaniments in the development of children's artistry also support and reflect the style and expressive import of the song, supporting vocal delivery at every level of development, without upstaging or overpowering children's voices.

An accompaniment that offers a piano introduction and interlude between repetitions of the song gives children the opportunity to perform a song they sing beautifully a second time, building confidence in their own artistry and giving the audience greater time to savor children's artistry at every level of development. Accompaniments that support the musical mind, the expression of song, and children's voices serve to illuminate both the musicality of the song and the wonder of children's artistry. (Piano accompaniments for songs presented in this chapter can be found in the Come Children Sing Institute SONG LIBRARY at www.comechildrensing.com/sl.php.)

**58**

**Figure 3.31**
Dorian, Multimetric—
Duple/Triple

**WHAT DOES LITTLE BIRDIE SAY?**

Let's take another look now at *What Does Little Birdie Say?* (Figure 3.31) presented earlier in this book with movement. See how you might view it differently in light of new awareness about how song architecture directs the musical mind, artistic expression, and vocal technique. What additional clues might you now find about its rhythm and tonal difficulty in relation to the musical mind? What new insights might you bring to the text of Alfred Lord Tennyson and how its setting relates to artistic expression and to vocal technique? How do you view the overall difficulty of *What Does Little Birdie Say?* in relation to the continuum of the development of children's artistry demonstrated in songs presented here? (Additional songs in various tonalities and meters that span this continuum are presented in Etude 3.)

Songs that give voice to children's artistry scaffold children's delivery musically, expressively, and vocally at every age and stage, developing the readiness for more advanced choral literature. Children who through multiple years have been supported by song to deliver line beautifully, to use the voice properly, and to express themselves in song, move into more advanced choral literature with experience building a line, articulating text, executing rhythm with momentum, shaping sound, creating a phrase, and breathing appropriately. They know what it feels like to be choral musicians, bringing a host of experience from a variety of songs that develop children's artistry through varying meters, tonalities, styles, tempos, texts, and difficulty levels. The skills are intact, ready to be applied to more difficult choral music. The excitement for the choral art and the motivation for ensemble singing are in place. The children are choral artists, with the readiness to take on choral music of the masters, complete with reverence for their greatness.

# 4

# Eliciting Artistry

Children's artistry is something we have to draw out of children, not something we can put into them. It is abundant, but it is shy, insecure, and vulnerable. Artistry is in every child, but it is not always accessible. Children are very protective of their artistry, hesitant to unveil its presence, expose its sensitivity, and reveal its hidden dynamic. Artistry is personal. Sharing artistry is intimate. Unmasking artistry among peers can be scary. Children's artistry maintains a protective shell, where it can quietly retreat at any time. The slightest threat to its fragile nature sends it inward.

Children's artistry, unveiled, is full of life. It is highly energetic, enthusiastic, and responsive. It is the vibrant life force of children engaged in making exciting music. Children's artistry seeks energy of its own kind to support and sustain its exuberance. It comes to life when it finds it, and withdraws when it does not.

Eliciting children's artistry is an art in itself. Musicality is irresistible for children's artistry, but how we prompt artistry either draws it out or sends it into its shell. Children's artistry is an expression of children's spirit. We have to address it with both reverence and vitality if we want to elicit its wonder. We have to honor its timid and fragile nature as we gently draw it out. We have to preserve, protect, and entice the vibrant life force of children, charging and sustaining its joyful energy with musical energy and with our own joyful energy. The willingness of children's artistry to unfold is dependent upon our creating a loving environment that is so musically compelling and so full of life that artistry cannot keep itself from becoming one with the music.

Children's artistry is propelled by children's energy. Well-meaning attempts to secure discipline often diminish the life force necessary to make music come alive. We cannot deflate children's spirit and expect artistry. We have to feed the spirit, nurture children's vitality, and celebrate life-giving musicality.

The energy, playfulness, and love of life that children naturally exude are essential to making exciting music, whether with children or professional musicians. The right notes at the right times with the right words, sung with proper vocal technique and decorum might produce a technically accurate performance, but that, alone, is not artistry. The vitality of the human spirit is necessary to breathe life into musical performance.

Children's energy in song and musical movement offers a good barometer of children's artistry, as children's energy both reflects and charges musical energy. Musicality is the greatest generator of the energy of children's artistry. Movement animates that energy. Our own liveliness, sense of humor, and playfulness feed that energy.

*Giving Voice to Children's Artistry.* Mary Ellen Pinzino, Oxford University Press. © Oxford University Press 2022.
DOI: 10.1093/oso/9780197606520.003.0005

Children mirror our vitality and enthusiasm for making exciting music. Their investment of artistry and their intimacy with musical nuance reflect our own. We have to make music come alive, which in turn, makes children come alive. We may, like many of the children, be shy and soft spoken in the classroom or rehearsal, but every musician becomes more energized, more compelling, and more vibrant in the process of making exciting music, eclipsing shyness, moods, and insecurities.

Living the energy that we want from children's artistry accelerates classroom pacing, which further increases energy. Slow pacing resulting from talking, inactivity, and tedium drains energy and shuts down artistry. Rousing musical energy with its faster pacing entices children's artistry, deters disruption, and motivates children to engage in making exciting music.

Some of us might be afraid to trust the power of children's artistry, fearing a loss of control of the children, the sound, or musical line. Children's artistry, when freed to be its most competent self, is highly focused, and it is excited to create a beautiful sound and expressive line. It feeds a collective sense of urgency among singers to deliver together even more beautifully. Our need for control often discourages children's artistry.

Some of us might be concerned that we wouldn't be able to sustain such vital energy through multiple classes or rehearsals. Eliciting children's artistry is exhilarating rather than exhausting. Teaching multiple classes without musical energy is far more draining. The more we engage musically and energetically with our children, the more we enliven and sustain children's energy, the more musically our children deliver, and the more vibrant we become as music teachers and conductors.

Enabling, sustaining, and empowering children's energy in the process of making exciting music is one of the greatest joys of teaching music. Children's energy brings to life the wonder of the music, and the music brings to life the wonder of children, weaving the two into one expressive whole. We cannot help but come alive ourselves in the process.

Children's artistry needs a positive, uplifting context that builds children's confidence in themselves as musicians. Children are as sensitive to our words, actions, and attitudes as they are to the music, as children are artists in life, attuned to every nuance. The slightest hint of criticism, intimidation, or implication of inadequacy can shut down children's artistry. It is difficult for any musician to sing with the breath of life when feeling deflated. Exposed artistry is vulnerable, heartened by ongoing support and appreciation of its efforts, whatever the age.

Sustaining children's artistry requires that we treat it with the dignity it deserves, demonstrate ongoing respect, and nurture vitality. Musicality has the greatest power over children's artistry, but our tender, yet energetic support and encouragement of the shy, yet vibrant artistry in every child is essential to eliciting children's artistry.

## Prompting the Musical Mind

Giving voice to children's artistry necessitates that we add techniques that speak to the musical mind. Cueing the wordless musical mind in sound makes our teaching more effective, while offering greater intimacy with the musical mind and a closer view of its idiosyncrasies.

Preparing the musical mind in sound for the meter and tonality of each activity and song empowers the musical mind to work most efficiently. The sound "prep" formats the musical mind to receive the meter and tonality to come. It aligns the musical mind with the particular meter and tonality, priming it to process the musical content that follows. Meter and tonality preps speak to all levels, facilitating the musical mind's understanding in sound of the unique characteristics of each meter and tonality, and the commonalities and differences across meters and across tonalities.

Meter and tonal preps suggested by Edwin Gordon are very effective.[1] A meter prep consists of a representative pattern of macro and micro beats that clearly defines the meter, followed by a couple of silent beats. Macro and micro beats in the chosen meter capture the musical mind and set up the chosen meter, guiding the musical mind to process the activity in that meter. The silent beats give the musical mind time to fully align with the meter. The prep can be delivered on a neutral syllable like "bah." Playing the prep on a drum to secure meter and tempo in the teacher's musical mind and then delivering the prep vocally to the children can be helpful. Figure 4.1 presents meter preps for four different meters, using just one possible beat grouping with each unusual meter. (See Appendix B for additional beat groupings.)

**Figure 4.1**
Rhythm Preps

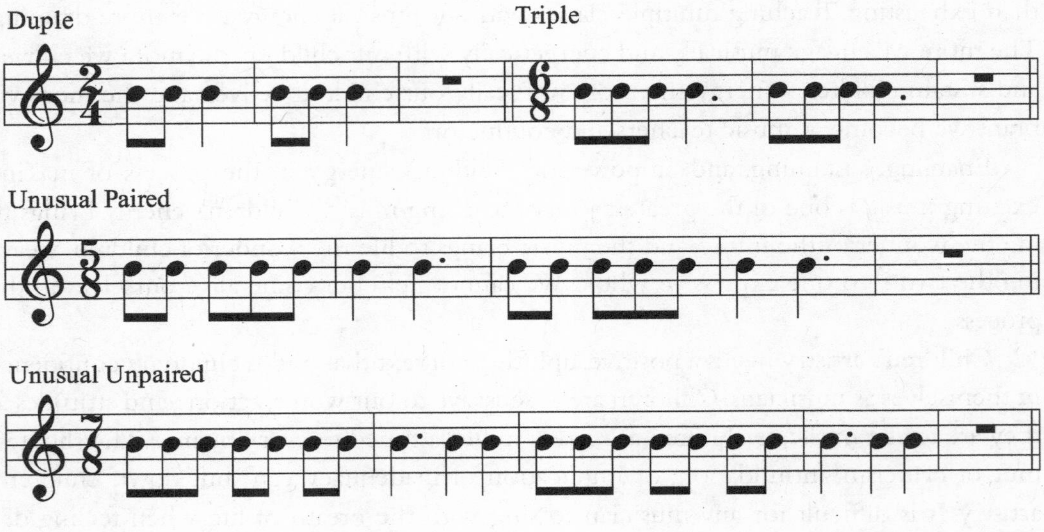

A tonal prep is the sequence of tones within the tonality, 5-6-5-4-3-2-7-1.[2] This sequence focuses the musical mind tonally and sets up the particular tonality, guiding the musical mind to process the activity in that tonality. The advantage of this particular sequence of tones over a scale in the tonality or tonic and dominant chords is in its arrangement of pitches in relation to the way the musical mind processes tonal. The sequence of tones revolves around and between the fifth and the resting tone, highlighting characteristic tones in each tonality in relation to the resting tone and fifth, securing tonality in the musical mind. Holding the resting tone longer than the other pitches gives the musical mind time to fully center in the tonality. The tonal prep can be delivered on a neutral syllable like "bah." Setting up the tonality for the teacher on a keyboard or other instrument and then delivering it vocally for the children serves well. Figure 4.2 presents tonality preps for three different tonalities with the same resting tone.

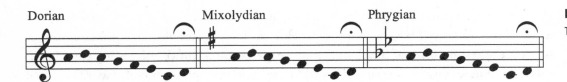

**Figure 4.2**
Tonal Preps

63

Rhythm and tonal preps seat the musical mind within the given meter and tonality, assuring growing competence with each activity or song to follow. They communicate to the musical mind what words cannot. They are sound cues, rhythm and tonal prompts. They encourage the musical mind to practice "mindfulness" of meter and tonality in the context to come. Rhythm and tonal preps used consistently to start each activity and song become shortcuts that speak directly to the developing sense of meter and developing sense of tonality at every level. They become code language with the musical mind to differentiate meters and differentiate tonalities, until the musical mind is sufficiently developed to associate its understanding of meters and tonalities with verbal labels. Rhythm and tonal preps often help teachers as well as children to secure the various meters and tonalities with greater assurance.

We can employ techniques that help keep the musical mind at the forefront of our classrooms. Singing on the resting tone of a song or activity, for example, anything that we might want to say to the children can deliver our verbal message in the context of tonality, without our words derailing the musical mind. We can also apply this technique when introducing a song with both a rhythm and tonal prep. Present the tonality prep, and then chant the meter prep in tempo on the resting tone, establishing tonality, meter, and tempo without the interruption of words.[3]

A simple technique that facilitates precise expression of the musical mind is the choice of neutral syllables with wordless rhythm and tonal activities. "Bah" works well for rhythm,[4] as it clearly articulates rhythm. Tonally, however, children sing better in tune on "too" than they do on the often used "bum" or other options. The tongue's pointed initiative of each pitch improves intonation of both children and teachers.[5]

The more we learn to speak to the musical mind, the more the musical mind speaks to us, exposing its musical needs. The musical mind is very willing to engage. We can suggest, if a group is reticent, that thinking minds suspend judgement while together we explore another capacity within the children that has no words, one for which the thinking mind cannot speak.

The fledgling musical mind moves its focus from meter to tonality or tonality to meter more easily than it does from one meter to another or one tonality to another. We can accommodate this tendency and hasten development by alternating rhythm and tonal activities, rather than presenting successive activities in two different meters or two different tonalities. An effective option is to present two or three successive rhythm activities in the same meter, or two or three successive tonal activities in the same tonality, shifting perhaps tempo or key between consecutive activities, but allowing the musical mind to stay within one meter or one tonality for more than one activity, intensifying its focus. The earlier suggestion to present a tonal narrative followed by a song in the same tonality exemplifies this technique, with the tonal narrative securing tonality in the musical mind for the song to follow.

The musical mind will navigate a change of key between consecutive tonal activities in the same tonality if we prepare the developing sense of tonality in sound. We might sing on the resting tone of the first, "Now we are going to move the resting tone here," singing the new resting tone on the word, "here," and then presenting the wordless tonal prep for that resting tone to establish the same tonality in another key. The words simply signal change. The musical mind will sustain the original tonality, now in the new key. The more developed musical mind can shift from one meter to another and from one tonality to another, cued by the prep of each different meter or tonality, but the separation of meters and the separation of tonalities in the early stages facilitate the development of a sense of meter and a sense of tonality.

The musical mind grows on contrasts—the contrast between meter and tonality, the contrast between meters, and the contrast between tonalities. The differences in beat groupings within the full spectrum of meters, and the differences in pitch relationships within the full spectrum of tonalities stimulate growth. Keeping all meters and tonalities alive in the musical mind propels children's artistry. Rotating meters through Duple, Triple, Unusual Paired, and Unusual Unpaired through successive class sessions, including at least two contrasting meters within each session, will better develop rhythm skills even in Duple meter, than focusing only on Duple meter, or focusing on just Duple and Triple. Rotating tonalities through Dorian, Mixolydian, Phrygian, Lydian, Aeolian, Major, and Minor through successive class sessions, including at least two contrasting tonalities within each session, will better develop skills in Major tonality than would focusing on just Major tonality or just Major and Minor. The suggested sequence of meters, ordered by difficulty, provides contrast between meters. The suggested order of tonalities alternates between those with a minor third and those with a major third, providing the greatest tonal contrast for the musical mind. (See Appendix C for contrasting tonalities.)

Learning to prompt the musical mind may lead to experimenting with techniques to further understand how the musical mind works. You might even discover a need to use words on occasion to deliberately break the intense focus of the musical mind, clearing the "aural palate" for another meter, tonality, or song. Teaching to the musical mind may be your greatest challenge in giving voice to children's artistry, but it will make the most profound change in your classroom or rehearsal, as the focused attention of the musical mind puts children in the palm of your hand and artistry within reach.

## Onward!

Giving voice to children's artistry is a growing process. Learning to teach to the musical mind takes time. Learning to use movement to generate musicality and energy takes time. Reviewing and selecting songs that inspire children's artistry takes time, and revising and developing techniques to elicit artistry takes time.

Children, too, need time to grow. Developing a sense of meter and a sense of tonality is an ongoing process. Some children may need more time than others to let go of the thinking mind and become expressive in song and movement. You cannot let yourself become discouraged if things do not progress as quickly as you might like, if something doesn't come out quite the way you had intended, or if children do not respond as you might have hoped. Determination to mine children's artistry and uncover the riches that lie within your own music classroom or children's chorus can keep you afloat, until the power of children's artistry sends you sailing.

Make your classroom your learning laboratory and start experimenting. Use your own brand of creativity and humor to become more unpredictable with your children, giving yourself greater latitude to try new things. Minimize your talking, energize your teaching, tweak practices that diminish artistry, and notice how each affects the children. Engage with the full variety of meters and tonalities and see how long it takes to capture the musical mind both rhythmically and tonally. Try a tonal narrative with movement followed by multiple repetitions of one of the short art songs in the same tonality and see how children respond. Use movement with songs or warm-ups you are already doing and observe how it affects musicality, sound, energy, and vocal technique.

Children will welcome your increased energy and positive feedback. They will embrace your making music come alive. They will engage with your energy in movement that expresses sheer musicality, and songs that inspire children's artistry. Children will revel in such energized musicality.

Giving voice to children's artistry necessitates ongoing reflection on our own teaching. Children do not deliberately sing unmusically. They mirror our teaching. Giving voice to children's artistry sometimes requires that we eliminate procedures that have defined our classroom or choral rehearsal, re-evaluate practices that have defined our field, and develop new techniques that serve children's artistry. Isn't it grand that something so musical can motivate us to grow as teachers and as a field?

Children's artistry strives for musicality, withdrawing from anything that is unmusical, lacking energy, or demeaning. Children innocently reveal the mystery of children's artistry in an ongoing manner as we learn to teach to the musical mind, engage in musical movement, employ songs that inspire children's artistry, and fine-hone our techniques.

Children's artistry is a precious gift to the music teacher and choral conductor. Children bare heart and soul to share this intimate dimension with us. Our time with the children may be the only time in their busy lives when artistry feels safe enough to reveal itself. Our setting may be the only musical context in which children ever experience their own artistry. We may be the only adults who ever engage with this side of the children, the only adults who embrace their energy, and recognize their potential as artists.

We can magnetize children's artistry. We can make our classes and choruses so inviting, so musical, and so full of life that children's artistry is compelled to come alive. We can transform every group of children we reach into a community of artists. We can give children's artistry wings to fly, as the wonder of the music and the wonder of children's artistry, together, can grow into a lifetime of making exciting music. We can empower children with their own artistry, propelled by the beauty of music and the beauty of their own souls.

Giving voice to children's artistry is essential in teaching music. We have in our hands the power to assure its preeminence in our classrooms and choruses—and in the field of music education. May the majesty of children's artistry illuminate the way.

**PART 2**

# Etudes

You are about to embark on an exciting journey, whatever level you teach, and whatever your preferred methodology. These Etudes can help you on that journey. They are designed to support you in the practice of giving voice to children's artistry. They provide a multitude of materials with guidance for direct implementation in the music classroom and children's chorus. They also provide professional development with tonalities and meters, movement, and song. Use these Etudes as needed to enhance your own growth, to amplify the material presented earlier, and to develop children's artistry.

"Etude 1-For Starters" is designed to help you reach and teach the musical mind. It offers songs and chants for tonal and rhythm narratives in the various tonalities and meters, with very short art songs that draw children deeper into tonality and into the choral art. This Etude can be applied in your music classroom or children's chorus for activities, recordings, or warm-ups. Etude 1 also provides for you to work independently with the various meters and tonalities as needed to develop greater competence and confidence in using them with children.

"Etude 2-For Movement" expands on material presented earlier and will guide you to apply movement specifically for momentum and the energy of the line in the classroom or choral rehearsal. It employs movement in a broad variety of musical challenges to propel momentum, capture musical nuance, and improve performance at every level. Songs and professional guidance in this Etude lead directly to use in the classroom or chorus, as well as providing the opportunity for you to work without children, as needed, in applying movement to music.

"Etude 3-For Songs" offers a wide variety of songs that give voice to children's artistry, clustered by difficulty. It will guide you in choosing songs that meet your children's musical needs through various levels of development. It will help you to select a comprehensive set of songs for each group of children that includes a variety of tonalities, meters, texts, expressions, and vocal challenges. The repertoire you choose in this Etude can be used in the classroom, children's chorus, and concert.

These Etudes will take you a long way on your journey. Additional songs and materials that meet the criteria of these Etudes, plus piano accompaniments for all the songs of Etude 3 and several of Etude 2 can be found in the Come Children Sing Institute SONG LIBRARY (www.comechildrensing.com/sl.php), where the songs are printable and searchable by various criteria, including tonality, meter, and difficulty.

*Giving Voice to Children's Artistry.* Mary Ellen Pinzino, Oxford University Press. © Oxford University Press 2022.
DOI: 10.1093/oso/9780197606520.003.0006

# Etude 1

## For Starters

A full palette of meters and tonalities feeds the musicianship of teachers and choral conductors as well as children. The musical richness of the various tonalities and meters can lead teachers and choral conductors to greater satisfaction in the classroom as musicians, whether with kindergarten or college singers. The joy of teaching and conducting multiplies when we can open to the greater depth of our own musicianship in the music classroom and choral rehearsal.

This Etude will guide you in capturing the musical mind and taking it on exciting journeys. It offers the opportunity for you to engage with the various meters and tonalities with or without children. It includes short musical examples for sustained time in each of the meters and tonalities. Both the materials and the presentation of those materials can be used directly in the music class or choral rehearsal for activities, recordings, or warm-ups.

Foundational materials that serve the development of children's artistry also serve music teachers and choral conductors who have limited experience with the various meters and tonalities. Many of us encountered modes and meters in music theory, but we didn't necessarily learn them in sound. Our adult musical minds are still ready for action, but we have to get our thinking minds out of the way so our musical minds can engage with meters and tonalities in sound and movement. We have to temporarily let go of music theory, notation, counting, imaginary keyboards, fingerings, or any other devices the thinking mind might try to employ to navigate meters or tonalities. We have to trust our own musical mind, as if it were a higher consciousness that can relate to music in a way the thinking mind cannot.

This Etude guides your thinking mind to provide for the musical mind, yours and the children's, so that you can all experience meters and tonalities in sound. The musical mind of all ages grasps meters and tonalities most efficiently through singing and movement, with the body navigating the current and the voice riding the waves. Engaging with this Etude with and without children will develop competence and confidence to use the various tonalities and meters effectively with children even if you have not previously had much experience with them. Insights gained from witnessing the process of your own musical mind in this Etude will inform your teaching.

Plan to focus on meters and tonalities for about 10 minutes at a time a couple of times a week for your own development or the children's, and at least 10 minutes weekly with children you meet only once a week. You may be stronger rhythmically or tonally

*Giving Voice to Children's Artistry.* Mary Ellen Pinzino, Oxford University Press. © Oxford University Press 2022.
DOI: 10.1093/oso/9780197606520.003.0007

but alternating between meters and tonalities will best serve your musical mind as well as that of the children. Two consecutive meters or two consecutive tonalities can confuse the musical mind that has limited experience in the less common meters or tonalities until the musical mind becomes secure enough to comfortably move from one meter to another or one tonality to another. Alternating between meter and tonality provides the time and space the musical mind needs to process each meter and tonality, which tend to remain in the musical mind after the live sound has ended. Engage in the full variety of meters and tonalities even if you feel competent in some of them. It is the contrast between those that are familiar to you and those that are not so familiar that will lead your musical mind to compare and contrast them in sound through its higher consciousness.

This Etude is designed in an ABA format, alternating meter and tonality, whichever you might be focusing on. Feel free to set it up as ABA, BAB, ABAB, or BABA for yourself or for the children, as long as you are alternating meter and tonality. Your ordering with the children might depend upon the time you have available, what you might have done in the previous session, or what song or activity might follow. You can also split up the pattern in a class with children, separating set AB from another set of AB or BA later in the class. The musical mind benefits from the contrast within a class session.

Consider the possibility of recording your sessions with this Etude for both you and the children. You could play them repeatedly for your musical mind while your thinking mind is busy driving the car, cleaning the house, or exercising. That will give your musical mind a chance to absorb meters and tonalities in sound without the interference of the thinking mind, notation, or instruments, each of which can distract the musical mind. You can also post the recordings online for your students to access when they are not in your music class or chorus, or for children who may come into your group late in the term without a background in meters and tonalities. You could even use the recordings in the classroom or choral rehearsal, engaging with the children and the recordings in singing and movement. Record each meter and tonality separately, so that you can mix and match meters and tonalities as needed.

Singing in tune in the various tonalities and chanting with appropriate weight distribution in the various meters can be a challenge for the teacher whose musical mind is not yet attuned to the various tonalities and meters. You can, if necessary, ask a colleague to record the musical examples for you, or you could record them on an instrument. Then sing and move with the recordings until you develop greater security vocally with each tonality and meter. Instrumental recordings can immerse the musical mind in tonalities and meters but singing and moving are necessary for the musical mind to fully engage with tonality and meter. Your children, too, can benefit from listening to the instrumental recordings, but a recording of your own voice singing in tune and chanting with appropriate weight distribution will activate the children's voices and bodies as you would in class.

You may find yourself and the children making great progress with meters and tonalities in just a few weeks. Don't be surprised if a tonality or meter pops into your head while you are going about your day. Welcome the unexpected visitor. Sing along, move along, or just let the musical mind continue to practice while your thinking mind is busy doing something else. You will also be practicing every time you engage in tonality and meter in singing and movement with children. The more the musical mind lives in the various meters and tonalities, the more the meters and tonalities will live in the musical mind.

## Meters

Figures 5.1 to 5.10 present two eight-bar chants in each meter. The first includes only macro and micro beats, and the second includes divisions. A secure sense of meter is anchored in macro and micro beats in each meter, with divisions of micro beats challenging the musical mind to sustain macro and micro beats even with minimal division patterns. There are, of course, many more difficult patterns in all meters. This Etude is intended for securing meter in the musical mind, rather than for developing a vocabulary of patterns in each meter. Security with macro and micro beats, with at least one division pattern in each meter, and with one beat grouping in the less common meters, provides the necessary foundation for everything more difficult.

Meters are presented here in order of difficulty. Combined meter is included, which was not introduced earlier in the book. Combined meter, like both Duple and Triple, has paired macro beats of the same duration, but one is divided into two micro beats and the other into three. A meter prep for Combined meter would sound like a prep for Duple with a triplet on one or the other macro beat. Children with a solid foundation in the four meters presented earlier readily handle Combined meter in chant and in song.

The design of the session presented here serves the development of both you and your children. The design and the materials can be directly used in the music classroom or choral rehearsal for activities, recordings, or warm-ups. Classroom application would, of course, be without verbalization, and could include tonguing as described in Chapter 2. The design of the session could also be used with more developed children to introduce more difficult patterns in each meter, always returning to macro and micro beats to secure the meter.

## In Practice

You are going to engage in a rhythm narrative, chanting and moving in a meter for two to three minutes, followed by a two to three minute segment with tonality as described in the next section, and then another two to three minute rhythm narrative in a contrasting meter. Chant on "bah" throughout the meters, with the kind of expression you might use with a favorite nursery rhyme—without discreet pitches, but with expression that makes your rhythm narrative interesting. Rotate meters through successive sessions so that they all get equal attention of the musical mind. Include one unusual meter in your contrasting pair until you feel enough security with each meter to pair more similar meters. Select your pair of contrasting meters and become familiar with the chants so you can let go of the notation as quickly as possible. Be sure to start each meter with a prep as described in Chapter 4. Keep the meter going throughout these four steps without losing a beat, and without notation as much as possible.

1. Chant the first chant in the meter twice through, engaging in flowing movement throughout. Use hips, knees, shoulders, and outstretched arms without regard to macro and micro beats.

2. Chant the first chant again and then the second chant in the meter, now with more gentle flowing movement that reflects greater awareness of macro and micro beats.

3. Chant the pair of chants again, this time engaging in macro and micro beat movement. Shift weight side-to-side on macro beats, while bouncing micro beats with the knees. Use full body weight, putting greater weight on macro beats.

4. Chant the pair of chants one more time, leaping into macro beats with full body weight while stepping micro beats throughout.

# Duple Meter

**Figure 5.1**
Duple, macro/micro

**Figure 5.2**
Duple, with divisions

# Triple Meter

**Figure 5.3**
Triple, macro/micro

**74**

**Figure 5.4**
Triple, with divisions

## Unusual Paired Meter

**Figure 5.5**
Unusual Paired, macro/
micro

**Figure 5.6**
Unusual Paired, with
divisions

## Unusual Unpaired Meter

**Figure 5.7**
Unusual Unpaired,
macro/micro

**Figure 5.8**
Unusual Unpaired, with divisions

# Combined Meter

**Figure 5.9**
Combined, macro/micro

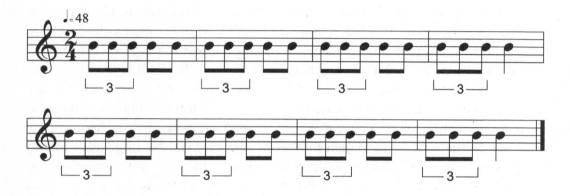

**Figure 5.10**
Combined, with divisions

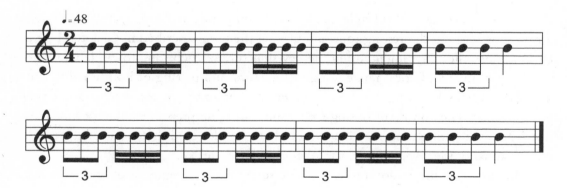

## Tonalities

Figures 5.11 to 5.24 present two short songs in each tonality. The first is without words, the second with words. The text of each song with words is a translation of a Japanese haiku. Each song without words will be used to create a tonal narrative from which the song with words can grow. The first song in each tonality secures the musical mind in the tonality, while the second challenges the musical mind to sustain the tonality with the addition of words and rhythm that reflect the expression of text.

The short songs, with and without words, are in the vocal range that serves the musical mind. The rhythmic simplicity of the songs without words directs the musical mind's attention to tonality, and the melodic contour of all the songs supports tonality in the musical mind. Sustained experience in short songs that serve the musical mind in each tonality provides the necessary foundation for voices to easily navigate the range that serves the vocal instrument.

Tonalities are presented here in the order recommended earlier in this book. You will gain the most from this Etude by using them in that order at least the first time through, as there is a particular challenge built in. Each pair of songs, except for one, shares the same tonality and meter, and they are in the same key. This facilitates a seamless transition between songs, with tonality dominating the experience, even if the songs are in different tempos. The song with words in Aeolian tonality is in a different key than the Aeolian song without words, requiring that you deliver an Aeolian prep for the song without words, and then another Aeolian prep for the song with words in the new key, both as described in Chapter 4. This will give you practice in setting up the tonality in a new key seamlessly, so that the musical mind sustains the tonality from one key to another. This may initially interrupt your musical mind's focus on tonality, leading you to greater awareness of why children's musical minds need the key change to be seamless.

Each of the songs in this Etude ends on the resting tone. You can create a tonal prep for each by locating the resting tone and playing the prep described in Chapter 4 on a keyboard or other instrument, using the key signature of each song to guide you. The narrow parameters of vocal range, song architecture, and pairing of both tonality and key within each set of songs limit the number of different resting tones across the seven pairs of songs. The consistent resting tones, and setting up preps for different tonalities from the same resting tone, may help you to better understand the characteristic tones of each tonality. (See Appendix C for Characteristic Tones.)

The design of the session presented here serves the development of both you and the children. It can be used in the music classroom or choral rehearsal for activities, recordings, or warm-ups. Classroom application would, of course, be without verbalization. The pairs of songs in this Etude can additionally be used to draw children into the choral art as described in Chapter 1. Any of the songs can also be used to secure tonality for a seamless introduction of any of the songs presented in Chapters 1, 2 and 3, or Etudes 2 and 3. The songs with words in this Etude could also be transposed up a third to use as warm-ups with children who have a background in tonalities and meters.

## In Practice

You are going to engage in a tonality in singing and movement for two to three minutes, followed by a meter segment as described in the previous section, and then another two to three minutes in a contrasting tonality. The experience with each tonality consists of a tonal narrative, and then a song with words growing out of that narrative. Rotate tonalities through successive sessions to keep them all alive in the musical mind. Include in your contrasting pair of tonalities one with a minor third and one with a major third, until you have the competence to pair more similar tonalities. The ordering of the tonalities here provides for that contrast. (See Appendix C for which tonalities have major or minor thirds.) Select your pair of contrasting tonalities and become familiar with the songs so you can let go of the notation as quickly as possible. Start each tonal narrative with a tonal prep as described in Chapter 4, using a piano or other instrument for the prep as needed. Keep the tonality going without verbal interruption throughout these three steps, and without notation as much as possible.

1. Sing the song without words at least twice through on "too" (more with children), engaging with flowing movement throughout. Use hips, knees, shoulders, and outstretched arms without regard to macro and micro beats.
2. Move seamlessly into singing the song with words at least twice through with flowing movement. (Change keys for the second song if necessary, using a tonal prep without interruption as described in Chapter 4)
3. Continue singing the song with words at least two to four additional times, now exploring the energy of the line in movement. Capture the drama of the song, with all its musical nuance. Continue to use flowing movement while using body weight as needed for weight in meter. Use arms and hands for building intensity, articulating words, or shifting styles. Continue movement through any rests, reflect the energy in the rhythm of the words, and explore the change in energy with any change of meter. Uncover greater musical nuance in movement with each additional repetition. Continue singing and movement until you alone, or you and the children get lost in sheer musicality.

**Figure 5.11**
Dorian, Duple

# Dorian Tonality

**Figure 5.12**
Dorian, Duple

# The Frog and the Cherry Petal

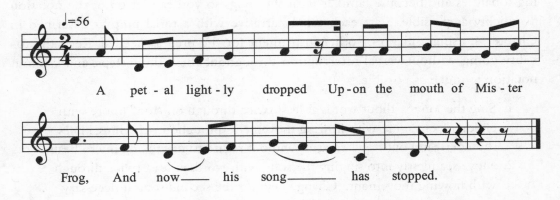

A pet - al light - ly dropped Up-on the mouth of Mis - ter

Frog, And now—— his song——— has stopped.

**Figure 5.13**
Mixolydian, Triple

# Mixolydian Tonality

# Fish in the River

**Figure 5.14**
Mixolydian, Triple

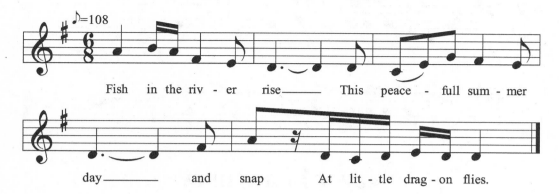

# Phrygian Tonality

**Figure 5.15**
Phrygian, Triple

# The Little Fly

**Figure 5.16**
Phrygian, Multimetric—
Triple/Duple

# Lydian Tonality

**Figure 5.17**
Lydian, Duple

# Never in a Hurry

**Figure 5.18**
Lydian, Duple

Ah, the but - ter - fly! ⎯⎯⎯

E - ven when chased it nev - er seems In a hur - ry. ⎯⎯⎯

# Aeolian Tonality

**Figure 5.19**
Aeolian, Duple

# Fluttering Butterflies

**Figure 5.20**
Aeolian, Multimetric—
Duple/Triple

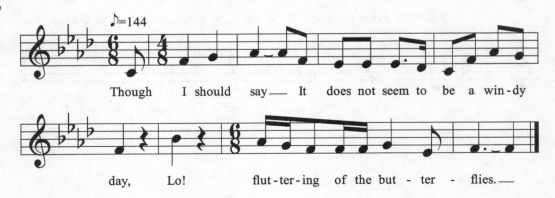

Though I should say ⎯ It does not seem to be a win - dy

day, Lo! flut - ter - ing of the but - ter - flies. ⎯

# Major Tonality

Figure 5.21
Major, Triple

# The New Year's Here Again

Figure 5.22
Major, Triple

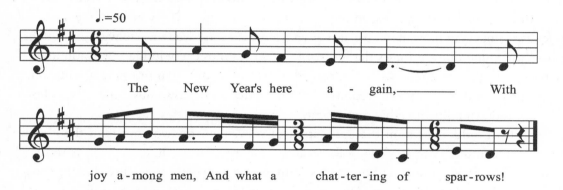

The New Year's here a - gain,_____ With

joy a - mong men, And what a chat - ter - ing of spar - rows!

# Minor Tonality

Figure 5.23
Minor, Duple

# The Pheasant

Figure 5.24
Minor, Multimetric—
Duple/Triple

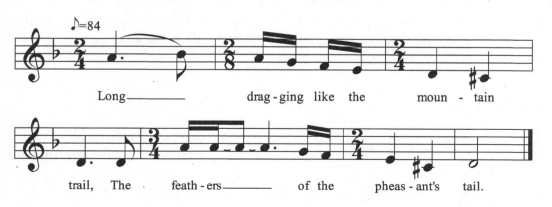

Long_____ drag - ging like the moun - tain

trail, The feath - ers_____ of the pheas - ant's tail.

# Etude 2

## For Movement

Learning to use movement to communicate musicality is an ongoing process. Rehearsing with movement provides instant feedback, so we learn from every attempt we make to engage singers in movement. We also learn from each song we rehearse with movement, as the unique musical forces that determine a song's musicality guide our communication through movement. We are informed still more by our own movement with song, as our embodiment of song prompts greater awareness of how music moves and how musical detail influences that movement.

This Etude focuses on the application of movement to two aspects of the choral art: momentum, with its driving force, and the energy of the line, with all its musical nuance. Artistry in the execution of these dimensions is essential to quality choral performance with singers of all ages. Applying movement in rehearsal to meter and to musical nuance makes momentum and the energy of the line come alive in song, improving performance at every level.

This Etude expands the material presented earlier in this book and offers a variety of musical examples for the application of movement to momentum and to the energy of the line, with or without children. Use this Etude as if you have only movement at your disposal to communicate musicality, giving you the opportunity to explore the direct connection between movement and the choral art. You can practice using movement in the music classroom and choral rehearsal, and you can practice alone in front of a mirror or solo video platform. Each setting offers the opportunity to explore movement in relation to the movement of the music, clarifying what type of movement a particular passage might need, guiding better communication through movement, and leading to improved performance with any choral literature and any ensemble.

Your children may or may not yet have experience with tonalities, meters, flowing movement, and macro/micro beat movement (See Etude 1). Assume for the purpose of this Etude that they have the readiness for the various musical challenges presented here. A tonal and rhythm prep with each example will be helpful for teacher and children of all levels (See Chapter 4).

## Momentum

The need for momentum in choral performance cannot be stressed enough, whether in day-to-day rehearsal or in concert. Our many attempts to improve rhythmic precision,

*Giving Voice to Children's Artistry.* Mary Ellen Pinzino, Oxford University Press. © Oxford University Press 2022.
DOI: 10.1093/oso/9780197606520.003.0008

expression, breath support, articulation, tempo, intonation, tone, or any number of musical concerns does not guarantee momentum in singing or performing choral music. Momentum is propelled by a solid underlying meter with appropriate weight distribution between macro and micro beats.

The change in momentum in the delivery of a song, following rehearsal for appropriate weight distribution between macro and micro beats, is dramatic. A music teacher who regularly facilitates that change will never view choral singing quite the same, whether conducting or in the audience. We as a field put so much emphasis on quality sound that we neglect the role of meter in generating momentum. Song, no matter how slow or ethereal, needs the vitality of momentum.

Rehearsal for momentum, with appropriate macro and micro beat weight distribution, engages singers in applying body weight to macro and micro beats simultaneously while singing. Standing and shifting full body weight on macro beats with up and down bouncing from the knees on micro beats activates appropriate weight distribution, with the heavier weight on macro beats being created by both the full body shift of weight and the bounce into it. This overstatement of weight distribution in meter, while singing, brings the developing sense of meter to the forefront of the musical mind in the context of song. It provides for singers to experience what it feels like to be mindful of macro and micro beats in song, and what it feels like to sing with momentum. This exaggeration of weight, seemingly unmusical, smooths out to become the more subtle feel of the underlying pulsing meter propelling momentum, whatever the level of the singers.

The soundness of the musical mind in song was compared earlier in this book to a tower of blocks, stacked from the bottom up with macro beats, micro beats, melodic rhythm, tonal, text, and then additional layers like accompaniments and parts. Any layer that is not secure can topple the tower, and the underlying rhythm blocks have to be solid to support the upper ones. Singers have to simultaneously process macro beats, micro beats, melodic rhythm, tonal, and text, plus our expectations for expression and vocal technique. The challenge of any one of these can distract from the others.

Song architecture directs the focus of the musical mind. Teachers direct children's attention to various dimensions in rehearsal, any of which can divert attention from macro and micro beats. The relationship between macro beats and micro beats becomes vulnerable in our stack of blocks. Every additional block adds greater pressure to the delicate balance between macro and micro beats, which is essential in order to perform melodic rhythm precisely. The musical mind has to be mindful of both macro beats and micro beats throughout, with appropriate weight distribution, for musicality and for momentum. Rehearsing a song with full body weighted movement on macro and micro beats strengthens the blocks in the tower that become most unstable when all the blocks are stacked, bringing mindfulness to both macro and micro beats, pacing melodic rhythm, and securing tempo.

Moving only macro beats or only micro beats in song is not enough to activate the underlying sense of meter to propel momentum. The musical mind requires both. Rehearsing for just macro beats or just micro beats does not embody the relationship between the two. Nor does it offer the experience of appropriate weight distribution which is necessary for musicality and momentum. Tapping or patting macro or micro beats, counting, talking about meter or momentum, or tapping heels or toes does not spark the developing sense of meter. Full body weight applied to macro and micro beats simultaneously in song ignites the musical mind, brings the developing sense of meter into the song, and propels momentum.

A lack of security with the relationship between macro and micro beats in song can manifest itself differently in different meters. The delivery of a song in Duple meter might sustain micro beats, but without appropriate weight on macro beats. The more difficult Triple meter seems to be the most tenuous in song with all ages and levels of experience. Singers often give weight to macro beats in Triple meter without pulsing micro beats, which generally results in a rushed tempo. It is the presence of micro beats in relation to the greater weight of macro beats that secures both meter and tempo.

Children often demonstrate greater momentum in song in one of the more difficult unusual meters than they do in the usual Duple or Triple meters. The weight of macro beats in unusual meters with their uneven number of micro beats seems to rivet the attention of the musical mind to meter more than the easier Duple or Triple meter. Ongoing exposure to the various meters with both flowing movement and macro/micro beat movement prepares singers to bring the developing sense of meter into song in any meter. Competence with any given meter in the context of rhythm does not guarantee the same level of competence with that meter in the context of song, with all the added layers. Rehearsing a song with full body weighted movement on macro and micro beats brings children's competence with a meter into the song, and then morphs into the more subtle feel of momentum.

*Grasshopper* (Figure 6.1), in Triple meter and Mixolydian tonality, invites rehearsal for the underlying meter in song with kindergarten and first grade singers. Song architecture establishes and reinforces the meter throughout with a melodic rhythm of primarily macro and micro beats and melodic contour and text that align with meter. Children naturally sway on macro beats as they get into the delight of this song, but often without regard to micro beats. Having the children sing the song with full body weight shifting on macro beats while knees bounce on micro beats will bring the weighted relationship between macro and micro beats into the song, securing tempo, improving articulation, and bringing new life to the grasshopper.

*Night* (Figure 6.2), in Dorian tonality and Triple meter, with its lovely text of Sara Teasdale, presents a more difficult challenge for the developing musical mind. Triple meter again provides the foundation, but the melodic rhythm is considerably more complex than *Grasshopper*, requiring singers to sustain the meter through long notes, rests, ties, and upbeats. The long notes offer particular challenge to sustaining momentum. Singing the song in rehearsal with full body weight shifting on macro beats while knees bounce on micro beats will bring the developing sense of meter into the song. *Night* is more demanding than *Grasshopper* not only with rhythm but also with text, expression, and vocal technique, all of which can distract the musical mind from macro and micro beats, particularly in Triple meter.

Rehearse a song for meter with appropriate weight distribution as often as necessary, just as you might rehearse regularly for articulation or expression. The musical mind can be distracted by any of the various layers on top of the foundation of meter. You might, for example, notice less clarity in meter when requesting attention to expression or breath. Children accustomed to rehearsing with weighted movement on macro and

# Grasshopper

**Figure 6.1**
Mixolydian, Triple

85

Grass - hop - per, Grass - hop - per, don't hop a - way.

I will not hurt you, I just want to play.

Grass - hop - per, Grass - hop - per, come take a chance.

Won't you show me how grass - hop - pers dance? We'll

hop, hop, hop,—— and hop—— to geth - er. We'll

hop, hop, hop,—— no mind to the weath - er.

Grass - hop - per, Grass - hop - per, don't hop a - way.

I will not hurt you, I just want to play.

*continued on next page*

**Figure 6.1**
Continued

Grass - hop - per,  Grass - hop - per,  come take  a  chance.

Won't  you  show  me  how  grass - hop - pers dance?  We'll

hop,  hop, hop,___  and  take___  our  stance,  For the

grass - hop - per,  hop - hop - per,  hop - per - grass  dance.___

**Figure 6.2**
Dorian, Triple

# Night

♪=105

Stars o - ver snow, And  in the west a pla - net  Swing - ing be - low a

star--  Look for a love - ly thing  and you will  find it,  It

is  not far--___  It  ne - ver will be  far.

micro beats often need only your swaying and bouncing a few macro and micro beats as a reminder. That starts their own motors running, bringing macro and micro beats to the forefront in the context of improving other dimensions of performance.

The next pair of songs (Figure 6.3 and Figure 6.4) presents a contrasting challenge amidst many similarities. Both songs are primarily in Unusual Paired meter. Both songs have only six measures. Both have a text that is a translation of Japanese haiku, and both songs are a dance. Yet each song invites a very different style, energy, and intensity in its dance. These compact little songs, through six to eight repetitions in singing and movement, offer the opportunity to address musical subtleties without the complexity of added length.

# A Pair of Butterflies

**Figure 6.3**
Dorian, Unusual Paired

*A Pair of Butterflies* (Figure 6.3), introduced in Chapter 3, demands appropriate weight distribution in a dance in Dorian tonality and Unusual Paired meter that is as light and smooth as the flight of a butterfly. Sing the song repeatedly, shifting full body weight on macro beats while bouncing micro beats, and letting the song gently float on top. See how smooth you can make the dance, yet with underlying momentum throughout, capturing greater musicality in movement with each repetition. Invite children who are familiar with this meter to sing and move with you and notice how beautifully they reflect the gentle dance amidst the unusual meter.

# A Lantern Dance

**Figure 6.4**
Minor, Multimetric—
Unusual Paired/Triple

*A Lantern Dance* (Figure 6.4) is a compelling little song in Minor tonality that develops greater intensity with each successive repetition. Don't let the key signature deter you. The final pitch is the resting tone. Just set up a prep for Minor tonality from that resting tone and go from there (See Chapter 4). The single measure in Triple meter adds gusto to the established Unusual Paired meter as it builds with the proclamation of the text. The quick tempo and repeated melodic figure throughout builds tension still more through multiple verses. Sing and move with this song through multiple repetitions. See if you can capture in movement through successive verses the drama of this little song, with its driving tempo, shifting meters, and melody that reflects the exciting dance. Invite children to sing and move with you and notice how much they get into the ongoing intensity and musicality of this little song. Multiple verses of this song create a haunting warm-up for all ages.

The fast tempo of this song, with its Unusual Paired meter, makes it difficult to bounce micro beats while shifting full body weight on macro beats. Unusual meters demand more of the musical mind than Duple and Triple meters. Children experienced with unusual meters in movement generally put weight on macro beats in unusual meters, with appropriate pacing of micro beats, even with tempos that are too fast to bounce micro beats. Rhythm in unusual meter is so compelling for the musical mind that the relationship between macro and micro beats cannot be sidelined as easily as it might be in the easier meters.

Children who have the rhythm readiness for a song in unusual meter with a tempo too fast to bounce micro beats are ready for a more advanced representation of meter in the context of song. Sing numerous repetitions of the song in the driving tempo, with appropriate weight on macro beats, and then on an occasional verse with everybody still moving macro beats, sing the melody in micro beats on "bah." Your weighted macro and micro beats on "bah" provide for children to hear micro beats in the melody in relation to the macro beats in movement when the tempo is too fast to bounce micro beats. This is, of course, all in flight, with the song ongoing at its original tempo, and without verbal commentary. Continue the song with another verse or two with text, and then intersperse a verse of chanting macro and micro beats on "bah" on the resting tone rather than on the melody. Your vocal demonstration of relative weight on macro and micro beats, while children continue to move macro beats, first strips the layer of text from the complex whole and then strips both text and melody, focusing the musical mind on the meter itself. Chanting on the resting tone keeps the tonality alive in the musical mind as if you are putting the melody on hold for a verse to tell the musical mind, "Listen to the meter of this exciting song. You know this meter." Sing a couple more verses with text to bring the song to a close.

Your chanting weighted macro and micro beats on "bah" on an occasional verse while singing the song shines an aural spotlight on meter for the musical mind in the context of song. It highlights both macro and micro beats with appropriate weight distribution amidst the layering of macro beats, micro beats, melody, text, and in this case, the fury of tempo. Children familiar with Gordon's rhythm syllables benefit still more from your chanting an occasional verse on the melody or on the resting tone with his rhythm syllables. The unique design of Gordon's rhythm syllables points out to the musical mind that knows them, not only the relationship between macro and micro beats, but also the change in meters and the identification of each meter. They can do all of this in the context of song, without verbal explanation.[1]

***Elephant*** (Figure 6.5), in Minor tonality, offers a longer and more difficult song in shifting meters. Unusual Unpaired meter shifts regularly to Triple and even Duple meter to accommodate the words. Its quick tempo makes it difficult to bounce micro beats. The weight of macro beats in the unusual meter with a quick tempo draws the attention of the

# Elephant

**Figure 6.5**
Minor, Multimetric—
Unusual Unpaired/
Triple/Duple

89

musical mind, with micro beats flying by. The mixture of unusual and usual meters in the sprightly tempo stimulates mindfulness of meter throughout. The musical mind won't ignore micro beats in this song even in the segments in Triple meter. The alignment of the words to the shifting meters aids children in placing appropriate weight on macro beats. Children's movement that captures the weight of macro beats throughout drives momentum in this song. The greatest challenge is in the final six measures amidst the shifting meters.

## Energy of the Line

The energy of the line is the impassioned life-force of musical nuance. It is the musical energy created by the coming together of every musical detail. It is the musical drama of the song that results from the intertwining of rhythm, melody, and text. It is the musical impact of a rest, an upbeat pattern, a consonant, ascending or descending pitches, repeated pitches or rhythms. It is the intensity, the capriciousness, the building, the resolution, the twisting and turning of line created by the unique musical detail of each song.

Movement that expresses the energy of the line embodies musical nuance. It is our means of communicating how this musical motive speaks, how this little rhythmic figure drives energy in the phrase, and how these long notes demand intensity. It is how we show our singers in the context of song, without verbalization, how this word has to be caressed, how this rest, repeated pitch, or tied note affects the musicality of the line, and how this passage or these words demand crisp delivery. It is how we communicate musicality through musicality.

Movement that expresses the energy of the line takes us beyond flowing movement and macro and micro beat movement, though it incorporates both. It breaks us out of beat patterns and takes us deeper into musical detail and how it impacts the energy of the song. We have used the weight of the lower body to propel momentum. Movement that most effectively communicates musical nuance is primarily with the upper body, through hands, arms, and shoulders. We as choral conductors regularly shape sound, shade vowels, and build lines with hands and arms. We can sculpt all dimensions of musical nuance, articulating words, twisting phrases, and shifting styles with our hands while arms maintain flow and shoulders lend appropriate weight to macro and micro beats.

Sculpting musical nuance with hands, arms and shoulders speaks to children's artistry. It draws children into the current of energy created by the musical detail of each song, as it comes alive in our movement. It entices children to ride the powerful waves of the choral art with us, twisting and turning with musical nuance. The ability of children of all ages to engage with musical subtlety in movement and singing far surpasses their ability to understand verbal explanations about musical detail or its impact on performance. Children with the musical readiness for a song, who rehearse musical nuance with movement while singing that song, sing with artistry—creating each line, articulating words, and driving rhythm, whatever the age or stage of development.

Our sculpting of musical nuance invites children to explore the energy of the line with their own musicality. We are communicating the energy of the line through movement without expecting children to move just as we do. One child might move with great sensitivity while another reflects our movement, and another demonstrates musical nuance in movement that we had not yet discovered. Children explore the energy of the line independently, yet in ensemble. Our model makes musical nuance more tangible for children and demonstrates the freedom to explore the energy of the line. Engaging our hands with our voices imprints musicality on our singers.

Three short musical examples follow (Figure 6.6, Figure 6.7, and Figure 6.8), each with the energy of the line created by the unique combination of musical forces in each song. Use these songs with or without children to explore the energy of the line in movement. The text of each of the three songs is a translation of Japanese haiku. Use the notation only to learn each song and then allow yourself to become the song in movement as well as in singing. Try sculpting musical nuance with your hands in each song through six to eight repetitions and see how much musical subtlety you can capture in movement. Let your hands move with the music, articulating every word and rhythm. Let your arms flow while shoulders lean into the weight of macro beats in relation to micro beats. Break out of conducting for the moment and sculpt the song as if it were a piece of clay, using hands, arms, and shoulders to create the tug and pull of every musical detail.

Note the difference in musical detail between the three short musical examples and see if your movement reflects those differences, using a mirror as needed. Explore movement through multiple repetitions of each of these songs. Experiment with various options with each of these songs until you feel your movement captures the musical nuance unique to each song.

# Butterfly Dreams

**Figure 6.6**
Dorian, Multimetric—
Duple/Triple

*Butterfly Dreams* (Figure 6.6), in Dorian tonality, with its shifting between Duple and Triple meter, presents an opportunity to discover movement for musical nuance through its brevity, simplicity, and musicality. Move your arms with flow and expression through macro beats and micro beats in the 4/8 section, using the shoulders to lend weight to macro beats. Use the hands to deliver the words on macro and micro beats in the 6/8 section, moving back to the flow of the final measure and repeated 4/8 section. Let your movement reflect the contrast between not only the change in meter, but also the simultaneous change in momentum, style, and text energy. Notice how the initial consonant of "butterfly" contributes to the energy in the shift of meter. Capture greater musicality in movement and singing with each repetition. Invite children to move with you through multiple repetitions, giving them hands-on experience with musical nuance as they become the song through singing and movement.

**Figure 6.7**
Lydian, Multimetric—
Triple/Duple

# Dreams of Flowers

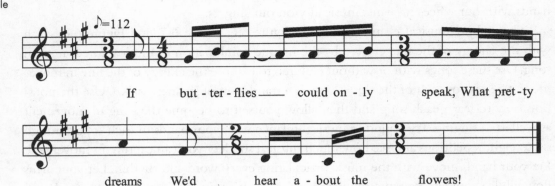

If but-ter-flies —— could on-ly speak, What pret-ty

dreams We'd hear a-bout the flowers!

*Dreams of Flowers* (Figure 6.7), in Lydian tonality, shifts between Duple and Triple meter with consistent micro beats. Use arms and hands in movement through multiple verses, playing with the energy created by the divisions of micro beats, in contrast to the longer notes throughout the song. Find the musical impact of each in movement and that of the tie. Use shoulders as needed to bring greater weight to macro beats. Let your arms and hands sing this song along with your voice, capturing the energy of the words, the restless flight through changing meters, yet the smoothness of consistent micro beats. Notice how the rhythm in relation to the sound of the words affects articulation and vowel focus. Find the commonality between lower body weight and upper body energy of the line. Capture greater musical subtlety with each repetition. Invite children to sing and move with you through multiple repetitions, allowing them to explore musical nuance through singing and movement, without verbalization.

**Figure 6.8**
Dorian, Triple

# Green Leaves in the Sunlight

Ah, how sub-lime-- The green ——

leaves, the young —— leaves In the light of the sun!

*Green Leaves in the Sunlight* (Figure 6.8), in Dorian tonality and Triple meter, captures the scene described with its statement of wonder. Use arms and hands to explore in movement the nuance of the expression in rhythm and melody through a number of repetitions of the song. Become the song. Sculpt the melody while singing, articulating the energy of the words with your hands, using arms to capture the intensity yet joy in the words. Use shoulders to lend weight to macro beats and feel their connection to lower body weight. Notice how the rest and upbeat patterns create energy that enables text expression with enthusiasm and awe. Create the song in movement just as you would like it to be sung with all its nuance. Let your body become an orchestrated symphony of musical energy while singing. Invite children to sing and move with you through multiple verses and notice how much musicality you are communicating without any verbalization.

The little art songs with texts translated from Japanese haiku that are presented in this Etude, in Etude 1, and in Chapter 1 offer multiple opportunities for you to explore in movement the impact of musical detail on the energy of the line. These little kernels of choral art through multiple repetitions enable artistry to bloom in singing and movement in singers of all ages. The brevity yet musicality of each of these little songs stirs artistry to feel through many repetitions how this word or that rhythm or a shift in meter affects the energy of the line. Singers of all ages discover greater musicality within each song and greater artistry within themselves, through each successive verse. The vocal range of these little songs serves the musical mind, without concern for vocal technique. Transposing any of these songs up a third for more developed singers makes a fine warm-up for any age to sing and move through multiple verses. Artistry aroused by such musicality is excited to apply itself to more advanced choral literature.

# Dreams

**Figure 6.9**

Dorian, Multimetric— Duple/Triple

*Dreams* (Figure 6.9), with the lovely words of Langston Hughes set in Dorian tonality with shifting Duple and Triple meters, offers a challenge for children ready for the musical, vocal, and emotional maturity of the song. It also presents a challenge for the teacher to make this song come alive with its slow tempo, shifting meters, and powerful message. Movement that communicates the energy of the line, with the contrast between the first and second halves of the song, leads children to sing this song with sensitivity and meaning. Movement with macro and micro beats, with the consistent micros throughout the shifting meters, propels momentum amidst the dramatic setting. Use rubato to accommodate the drama of the text through shifting meters. Articulate with hands and arms the powerful text, capturing its drama in movement. Notice if there is a difference in your movement with the repeated figure on "Life is a," as each leads to a very different energy of the line. Notice your repeated delivery of the word "dreams," each time on the same pitch, but each time moving to a different energy. See how differently the initial consonants and vowel sounds in the words "die" and "go," following the word "dreams," might affect the energy of the line. Notice the impact of the triplets, the thirty-second notes, and the long notes on the energy of the line. Sing and move through this song through several repetitions, rehearsing your own movement to capture the unique musical expression of this song. Then invite children to sing and move with you, inspiring the depth of artistry in singers ready for this challenge.

Communication of the energy of the line through movement that embodies musical nuance includes the underlying pulsing of meter. Teachers as well as children bring a greater feel of meter with appropriate weight distribution to upper body movement as a result of rehearsing for momentum with the lower body. Regularly applying movement in rehearsal for momentum and for the energy of the line at every level will also excite performance in the songs presented in Chapter 2, Chapter 3, and Etude 3, and will improve the performance of any choral literature. You will know by your ensemble's delivery of song whether or not your singers are weighting macro and micro beats and how well you have communicated musical nuance in movement. Tweak movement accordingly and continue to rehearse with movement whatever is still lacking. The more children rehearse with movement the more they embody musicality and the less they need such overt movement from you. Conducting in concert may need only the addition of an occasional well-placed cue to activate the feel of movement rehearsed with a particular song or passage.

Let's now revisit **Autumn Thought** (Figure 6.10) presented in Chapter 3, with the poem of Langston Hughes set in Minor tonality and Triple meter. Ask yourself the following questions about using movement to rehearse this song for momentum and energy of the line, reflecting on insights you have gained from this Etude.

1. How might you assure the foundation of Triple meter throughout this song, complete with appropriate weight on macro and micro beats to propel momentum?

2. How might you use your hands, arms, and shoulders to communicate desired articulation of the words "happy" and "summer" in the context of the first line to evoke the expression of the words, their rhythmic impact, and their joy, while sustaining the weight of the meter?

3. How might you express through movement the greater intensity of the second line in relation to the first, and how might the long note play into that?

4. How might your movement on "dry and withered" express the momentary despair at the peak of the song, the flow, yet the weight of meter?

5. How might your hands and arms express the joyous dance of the petals in contrast to "dry and withered?"

# Autumn Thought

**Figure 6.10**
Minor, Triple

# Etude 3

## For Songs

Music teachers and choral conductors are always in the process of selecting songs for children. We regularly serve the same children through multiple years, requiring that we choose a fresh set of songs for each group of children every term throughout consecutive years. A set of songs that give voice to children's artistry—songs that compel the musical mind, prompt artistic expression, and enable vocal technique—through progressive levels of development move children of all ages and stages forward as choral artists every term.

This Etude offers the opportunity for you to select for your own children sets of songs that give voice to children's artistry. A variety of songs that compel the musical mind, prompt artistic expression, and enable vocal technique are presented here in three clusters spanning the continuum of song difficulty introduced earlier in this book and serving a broad range of ages and stages. Each cluster of songs includes a variety of tonalities, meters, texts, styles, expressions, and vocal challenges, with each successive cluster generally more difficult. Musical, expressive, and vocal considerations are addressed for each song throughout the spectrum of difficulty, helping you to choose songs that meet your children's musical needs, while an accompanying Song Selection Guide facilitates the process. Your challenge is to choose for your children a comprehensive set of five songs that includes four to five different tonalities, three to four different meters, and a variety of texts, expressions, and vocal challenges. You can choose songs presented earlier in this book as well as those presented in this Etude.

The overall difficulty of any given song is dependent upon its unique combination of musical challenges. Consider each song's rhythm, tonal, expressive, and vocal dimensions, and choose a combination of songs that both challenge and support your children's developing artistry. One song, for example, might challenge your children's vocal technique or expression while supporting a developing sense of meter and tonality. Another might challenge your children rhythmically or tonally while reinforcing vocal technique and generating expression. A well-balanced combination of songs can stretch your children rhythmically, tonally, expressively, and vocally while empowering your children's developing artistry.

Songs presented here are loosely clustered by overall difficulty, with some overlap between clusters, various combinations of difficulty within each song, and a range of difficulty within each cluster. Let your children's musical needs guide you in selecting sets of songs for multiple groups of children at various ages and stages. You may have a group of children that straddles adjacent song clusters. You may have a chorus with multiple ages and experience levels. You may have children who first need extended experience

*Giving Voice to Children's Artistry*. Mary Ellen Pinzino, Oxford University Press. © Oxford University Press 2022.
DOI: 10.1093/oso/9780197606520.003.0009

with the various tonalities and meters, as provided in Etude 1, to develop the musical readiness for these songs. Your review and selection of multiple songs that give voice to children's artistry at progressive levels of development will guide you in choosing songs for every group of your children every term as they grow through ages and stages.

The comprehensive set of songs you select for your children, with multiple tonalities, meters, texts, expressions, and vocal challenges, will serve the development of children's artistry in both the music classroom and choral rehearsal. Children at every level with the musical readiness for the songs you choose will easily learn them through intimacy with the choral art in singing and movement, without piano accompaniments, without notation, and with tonal and rhythm preps as described in Chapter 4. Rehearsal for momentum and the energy of the line, addressed in Etude 2, can improve performance of these songs at all levels. Children who learn to sing your set of songs beautifully are then ready to rehearse them with piano accompaniments, creating a concert program awaiting an audience. Piano accompaniments for all the songs presented in this Etude can be found in the Come Children Sing Institute SONG LIBRARY (www.comechildrensing.com/sl.php).

## Song Selection Guide

✓Checklist for Each Song

|  | 1. | Are the rhythm challenges appropriate for my children's rhythm development? |
|---|---|---|
|  | 2. | Are the tonal challenges appropriate for my children's tonal development? |
|  | 3. | Are the text and expressive import of the song appropriate for the age of my children? |
|  | 4. | Are the vocal range and required vocal technique appropriate for my children's vocal development? |

|  |  | Song Choices | Tonality | Meter |
|---|---|---|---|---|
|  | 1. |  |  |  |
|  | 2. |  |  |  |
|  | 3. |  |  |  |
|  | 4. |  |  |  |
|  | 5. |  |  |  |

✓Checklist for Each Set of Songs

|  | 1. | Does my set of songs include 4 to 5 tonalities? |
|---|---|---|
|  | 2. | Does my set of songs include 3 to 4 meters? |
|  | 3. | Does my set of songs include a variety of texts, styles, expressions, and vocal demands? |
|  | 4. | Does my set of songs sufficiently challenge yet reinforce my children's developing artistry, rhythmically, tonally, expressively, and vocally? |

(Print Song Selection Guide at www.comechildrensing.com/ssg.php.)

### Song Cluster 1

The first cluster of songs serves the musical, emotional, and vocal needs of inexperienced singers who are familiar with the various tonalities and meters. These songs are appropriate for kindergarten and first graders as well as for older, inexperienced singers. Songs at this level also serve well as warm-ups for more developed children. Each of these songs, in its own unique way, compels the musical mind, prompts artistic expression, and enables vocal technique. Use the Song Selection Guide to help you in selecting a comprehensive set of songs at this level that meets your children's musical needs.

**Figure 7.1**
Mixolydian, Duple

# A Merry Sparrow

*A Merry Sparrow* (Figure 7.1), with the text of an English rhyme set in Mixolydian tonality and Duple meter, offers a delightful little song that can charge energy with all ages. Building intensity through the long notes and the peak of the second phrase is exciting for singers. Both tonality and meter are clearly defined within the first couple of measures of this song. The long notes offer rhythm challenge, yet they can drive musicality in this song, with underlying macro and micro beats propelling intensity and momentum through those long notes. The upbeat patterns add a bit of rhythmic challenge. The melody wraps around and between the resting tone and fifth, with rhythm and tonal together reinforcing rhythm anchors, tonal anchors, and the characteristic seventh of Mixolydian that defines the tonality (See Appendix C for Characteristic Tones). The simple text with its repetition aligns with rhythm and tonal anchors, and the vocal range is optimal for children's voices. Melodic contour supports expression, with the second line building marvel at this little bird, as well as expression and vocal technique. Driving energy in wonder of the merry bird drives energy in merry singers. Tonal and rhythm preps prepare the musical mind for the song's tonality and meter while movement with this song enlivens the body and the song. Children's artistic delivery of this song makes the song come alive with the joy of children as well as sheer musicality.

# Turtle

**Figure 7.2**
Aeolian, Triple

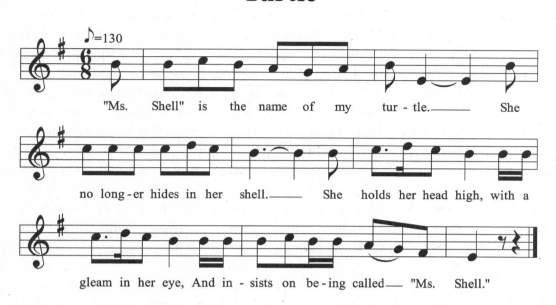

"Ms. Shell" is the name of my tur-tle.——— She no long-er hides in her shell.——— She holds her head high, with a gleam in her eye, And in-sists on be-ing called— "Ms. Shell."

*Turtle* (Figure 7.2) offers a more pensive expression than *A Merry Sparrow*. Aeolian tonality and Triple meter set the stage for a bit of a tribute to the admirable turtle for her independence and confidence, drawing much the same qualities out of young singers. Both meter and tonality are defined within the first few measures. A closer look at song architecture shows a bit of tricky rhythm in Triple meter with the dotted rhythms, ties, and upbeats. The Aeolian melody supports the musical mind tonally, poised around and between the resting tone and fifth with a lot of stepwise passages. The text aligns with rhythm and tonal anchors. Vocal placement encourages breath support and quality tone, with the melody hovering around the voice break. Melodic contour, with the underlying macro and micro beats of Triple meter, help to express the text, enabling children to present their story with great pride. Tonal and rhythm preps set children on the right track with this song, while movement for momentum and the energy of the line make this song a delightful addition to any class, rehearsal, or concert.

# Lie A-Bed

**Figure 7.3**
Mixolydian,
Unusual Paired

Lie a-bed, Sleep-y head, Shut up eyes, bo - peep; Till—

day - break Ne-ver wake: Ba-by, sleep.———

*Lie A-Bed* (Figure 7.3), with the lovely words of Christina Rossetti set in Mixolydian tonality and Unusual Paired meter, draws uncommon artistry out of young singers who have the musical readiness for this song. The unusual meter gives this seeming lullaby rich food for the musical mind. Children need some facility with Unusual Paired meter to competently sing this song. The opening with an upbeat pattern adds greater rhythmic challenge, as does the dotted quarter note macro beats without corresponding micro beats in the first few measures. Tonal challenges include the opening on the third, with the characteristic seventh of Mixolydian appearing well before the resting tone (See Appendix C for Characteristic Tones). Melodic contour flows between and around the resting tone and fifth with plenty of stepwise passages. Rhythm and melody align with text, supporting the meter, tonality, and text. Vocal placement is appropriate for young singers, with much of the song hovering around the voice break. This song draws a lovely sound from children as melodic contour shapes expression. A couple of slurs stretch vocal technique, as does phrasing. Rhythm and tonal preps serve to seat children in the meter and tonality without ambiguity. Note that the prep for the unusual meter of this song would be with the beat grouping 3–2 that prevails in this song (See Chapter 4). Rehearsing with movement sustains meter, propels momentum, and reinforces all other dimensions. Children's artistry glows through this lyric little song.

*Parakeet* (Figure 7.4) offers a fun challenge in Lydian tonality and Duple meter. The rhythm of the song is relatively easy, and both Duple meter and Lydian tonality with its characteristic fourth are defined in the first couple of measures. The melodic contour facilitates delivery with its stepwise passages, its revolving around and between tonic and dominant pitches, and its reinforcement of Lydian's characteristic fourth. The ascending and descending lines of this song, however, can be a challenge for both the children and the teacher who are not secure in Lydian tonality. A tonal and rhythm prep helps greatly, but also preceding this song with the Lydian songs of Etude 1 will better assure that children and teacher will be securely in Lydian tonality. Singers might otherwise tend toward the more familiar Major tonality, singing the fourth flat (See Appendix C for Characteristic Tones). Tonal, rhythm, and text align in support of each other, and the story of the parakeet with its play on words encourages expressive delivery with clean articulation. Vocal placement of this song is appropriate, offering word play around the voice break. This song evokes a very nice sound from children's voices as Lydian often does. Movement of the lower body in the context of rehearsal of this song secures meter with momentum. Movement of the upper body with sculpting hands, as described in Etude 2, produces clean articulation while capturing the whimsical story that children delight to tell. Children enjoy the play with words in this song, but take their own musicality more seriously, singing this song with the artistry of choral musicians.

*Butterfly* (Figure 7.5), in Phrygian tonality, presents a gentle, yet robust challenge for children with the rhythm readiness for a song in Combined meter. Both meter and tonality are well defined and reinforced throughout. The arpeggiated and repeated opening line outlines the harmonic functions that define Phrygian with its characteristic second (See Appendix C for Characteristic Tones). Rhythm and tonal in this song

# Parakeet

**Figure 7.4**
Lydian, Duple

101

support each other and align with text in support of Combined meter and Phrygian tonality. The single slur challenges a bit more rhythmically and vocally. Introducing this song with tonal and rhythm preps sets up the musical mind for the tonality and meter. The meter prep for this song would be much like the prep for Duple, but with a triplet on the second macro beat. Children with some competence in Combined meter will easily handle the later switches of beat groupings to 3–2 and back, though both the meter and the varying beat groupings add rhythm difficulty. The easy text of the first half of the song with its play on words becomes more sophisticated in the third line, increasing the song's difficulty still more, despite the fourth line's repetition of the first. Movement secures both meter and momentum. The children and the butterfly hover easily in the opening line and its repetition. They try their wings in the third line, which sends the butterfly and children's voices soaring, evoking greater breath, momentum, and expression, and drawing a lovely sound from children. The butterfly and children's artistry take wing in this song with elegance.

**Figure 7.5**
Phrygian, Combined

# Butterfly

Lit-tle But-ter-fly, won't you flut-ter by? Lit-tle But-ter-fly, flut-ter by me.

Lit-tle But-ter-fly, won't you flut-ter by? Lit-tle But-ter-fly, flut-ter by me.

Spread your but-ter-fly wings, flut-ter by things That beck-on your grace - ful flight.

Lit-tle But-ter-fly, won't you flut-ter by? Lit-tle But-ter-fly, flut-ter by me.

**Figure 7.6**
Mixolydian, Unusual
Unpaired

# Dancing Girl

There's a lit - tle girl who's danc - ing,—— Danc-ing to the

beat.—— But she does - n't wear her shoes for danc-ing, She

just wears her feet.—— But she does - n't wear her

shoes for danc-ing, She just wears her feet.——

*Dancing Girl* (Figure 7.6), in Mixolydian tonality and Unusual Unpaired meter, offers sheer joy with the grace of a dance. The song requires some competence with the difficult meter as upbeat patterns and ties increase rhythmic difficulty. The interesting rhythm will upstage tonal in this song, so the musical mind has to sustain Mixolydian tonality amidst the compelling rhythm. The vocal range serves children's voices at this level, while melodic contour supports Mixolydian tonality as well as Unusual Unpaired meter and the pronunciation of text. The melody intensifies the dance and expression of this song with the higher second phrase, moving back to a comfortable dance in the unusual meter. Tonal and meter preps help to secure the meter and tonality for children while movement with the song enhances meter, expression, momentum, and the energy of the line. Note that the rhythm prep for this song in Unusual Unpaired meter would be with the beat grouping 3–2–2 (See Chapter 4). Kindergarten and first graders delight in the text. Its simplicity and repetition add to the ease of this song with children who have the necessary musical readiness. The smooth lightness of the song reflects the joy of the text and the joy of the children, evoking dancing voices.

Additional songs in this book that fit into this cluster of difficulty include *Where Are My Roses?* (p. 41), *Dance to Your Daddy* (p. 39), *Ant* (p. 46), *In Spring the Birds Do Sing* (p. 50), and *Grasshopper* (p. 85). Children who competently sing your comprehensive set of five songs at this level are ready to rehearse them with piano accompaniments, creating a well-balanced concert program. You can further broaden the number of tonalities or meters at this level by using as warm-ups any of the little art songs with translated haiku texts presented in Chapter 1, Etude 1, and Etude 2.

## Song Cluster 2

This cluster of songs generally demands greater musical, emotional, and vocal maturity than those of the first cluster, compelling the musical mind, prompting artistic expression, and enabling vocal technique with more developed singers. These songs serve children with a background in tonalities and meters who have experience with songs that give voice to children's artistry at the easier level. The texts and musical challenges suit a broad range of ages. These songs also serve well for warm-ups with more developed singers. Use the Song Selection Guide that accompanies this Etude to help you in selecting a comprehensive set of songs at this level that includes a variety of tonalities, meters, texts, expressions, and vocal challenges.

*Two Children* (Figure 7.7) presents the delightful text of Elizabeth Barrett Browning challenging children to narrate a story while playing a practical joke in Major tonality as it shifts between Duple and Triple meter. Elongation and upbeat patterns add greater difficulty. So do ties, as well as the rests in the final 3/4 measure which are critical to the drama of the story. Melodic contour revolves around and between the resting tone and fifth, but with a number of wide skips. Rhythm and tonal challenges mirror the expression of the text. Rhythm anchors, tonal anchors, and text are in alignment, supporting each other. The

# Two Children

We were two chil-dren small, Mer-ry by child-hood's law; We used to crawl to the hen-house— And— hide our-selves in the straw. We crowed like cocks and when-ev-er The pass-ers near us drew, "Cock-a-doo-dle!" they thought——— 'Twas a real— cock that crew!

range serves young voices well, but the broader skips and slurs offer vocal challenge. The text requires greater maturity than those of the earlier cluster, as it is longer, and its poetic language is more sophisticated, requiring articulation to match. The greatest challenge of this song is in expression, with children narrating the story and then becoming the children crowing like cocks to fool onlookers. The complex rhythm of this song, plus the tonal, text, vocal, and expressive challenges, require readiness in multiple dimensions. Meter and tonality preps help to assure security in Duple meter and Major tonality amidst the many musical challenges. Movement with this song enhances momentum, energy of the line, and the telling of this charming story. Delivering this story makes children come alive while children make the story come alive, charming all with such cleverness and artistry.

*Yak* (Figure 7.8) captures children's sense of humor as well as the musical mind. The setting in Dorian tonality and Unusual Unpaired meter offers a fun little romp for children of most any age.

# Yak

**Figure 7.8**
Dorian, Unusual
Unpaired

105

What do you know a - bout— the yak? Does it cluck, or bark, or

moo,— or quack? Does it have a trunk or hump on its back?

What do you know a - bout— the yak? 2. Here's what I know a -

bout— the yak. It does - n't bark, or moo,— or quack. It

has no trunk or hump on its back. That's what I know a - bout— the yak.

Meter and tonality are defined in the first few measures. The challenging meter draws attention to itself while the humorous text draws its own attention. The musical mind has to hold its own tonally amidst such compelling distractions. Rhythm, tonal and text support each other, with melodic contour supporting the musical mind and the voice. The occasional slurs stretch vocal technique just a bit. The energy of the line supports expression with it building to the peak of each verse with successive questions or answers. The second verse fosters both confidence and delight as children deliver such profound answers to their questions. Introducing this song with a tonal and rhythm prep prepares the musical mind for the tonality and meter. Set up the meter prep in Unusual Unpaired meter with the beat grouping 3–2–2, which is consistent in this song (See Chapter 4). Rehearsing the song with movement will secure meter, energy, and momentum. Children with the musical readiness for this song will proclaim with authority, artistry, and a twinkle in the eye their extensive knowledge about a yak.

*Autumn Dusk* (Figure 7.9) presents the lovely text of Sara Teasdale in Minor tonality and Triple meter, which are established in the first few measures. This song demands security in the underlying meter, particularly on the long notes without the melodic rhythm pulsing micro beats. The upbeat pattern in the final line adds to rhythm difficulty. Melodic contour supports tonality, rhythm, and text, adding a bit of tonal difficulty

**Figure 7.9**
Minor, Triple

# Autumn Dusk

I saw a-bove a sea of hills A sol - i - tar - y plan - et shine, And there was no one near or far To keep the world from be - ing mine.____

by starting on the fifth. The greatest challenge of this song is with expression and vocal technique, especially in building energy on the longest note and navigating the leap in the final proclamation. The vocal range of this song draws the best out of children's voices, as the energy of the line increases in intensity to the peak of the song. The expression of the final line with its octave jump, enhanced by hand and arm movement for musical nuance, enables appropriate vocal technique as well as the meaningful expression of text. Sara Teasdale's tender words invite children to engage with the wonder of their own imaginations and their own artistry. Introducing this song with tonal and rhythm preps will lead the musical mind to the appropriate tonality and meter for this song. Movement in rehearsal will secure meter, tempo, momentum, and energy of the line. This song inspires such choral artistry that it is hard to believe that the singers are the same children who first walked into your room.

*Giraffe* (Figure 7.10) presents a grand musical challenge in Dorian tonality shifting between Triple and Duple meter. The shifting of meter is just the tip of the iceberg of rhythm difficulty. The long notes increase difficulty, demanding pulsing macro and micro beats underneath, as do the rests and very short pick-up notes which reflect the pronunciation of the word giraffe. The slow tempo adds still greater difficulty. Neither tonality nor meter is established immediately, increasing the difficulty of the song and increasing the need for tonal and rhythm preps. Additional tonal difficulty includes starting on the fifth, as well as the characteristic sixth of Dorian tonality not appearing until late in the song (See Appendix C for Characteristic Tones). Rhythm, tonal, and text support each other, but rhythm and tonal challenges require substantial readiness. The repeated motive on the word giraffe creates a holding tension that frames the pondering about the long features of the giraffe. Melodic contour enables expression and appropriate vocal technique for the melismatic passages with increased breath for each one. Vocal range of the song is comfortable for young singers, as is the text, but the musical and vocal needs of this song can challenge some of the most advanced singers. Rehearsal with movement

# Giraffe

**Figure 7.10**
Dorian, Multimetric—
Triple/Duple

107

is essential to drive momentum with weighted macro and micro beats through the long notes and through the long melismatic lines. Children with the readiness for this song rise to the height of artistry, reaching the height of the giraffe.

*Seahorse* (Figure 7.11), in Mixolydian tonality and Combined meter, is a jewel in the repertoire. The song captures children's imagination and delivers pure artistry. Rhythmic difficulty includes Combined meter with its contrasting division of micro beats into two and three. Meter and tonality are set up in the first measures and sustained throughout. The melody starts on the third, adding a bit of tonal difficulty, while rhythm, tonal, and text support each other. The text, though seemingly easy, offers a bit of challenge in ordering the similar three-syllable adjectives. Melodic contour aligned with Combined meter encourages expression and phrasing. The energy of the line builds with each statement about the seahorse, unveiling its wonder with greater and greater intensity, enabling the necessary vocal technique to deliver each line with appropriate breath support. The weight of macro beats on each of the adjectives about the seahorse supports a deliberate approach to each of those adjectives, while pulsing micro beats in this meter support articulation. The combination of these factors, set in the vocal range where children's voices ring, makes this song draw a lovely sound from children. Tonal and rhythm preps will help to assure that the

**Figure 7.11**
Mixolydian, Combined

# Seahorse

Sea - horse, del - i - cate    sea - horse.——    Sea - horse, beau - ti - ful

sea - horse.——    Mag - i - cal sea - horse,    grace - ful sea - horse.

Fan - ci - ful,    frag - ile,    sea - horse.———

musical mind is in the tonality and meter to receive this song, and weighted movement on macro and micro beats in Combined meter will secure both meter and momentum. The prep for Combined meter would be with the micro beat grouping of 2–3 for the opening, with macro beats of equal length. Children with some competence in the meter will have no problem with the shift of the beat grouping to 3–2 later in the song. This song captures the delicate presence of both the seahorse and the children.

*Dolphin* (Figure 7.12), in Dorian tonality with its shifting unusual meters, presents a musical challenge that captures the smooth, unexpected grace of the dolphin as it soars through the water, jumping at will. The shifting meters are as smooth as the dolphin despite moving between Unusual Paired and Unusual Unpaired meters, with the occasional Triple meter. The agitation of the unusual meters is increased by the rests and by the shifting beat groupings in both unusual meters. Children need considerable readiness for this song to be able to sustain Dorian tonality amidst the complex rhythm. Rehearsing with movement will facilitate meter, momentum, and the energy of the line. The melody supports the musical mind and reflects the shifting meters, with both rhythm and tonal mirroring the text as well as the dolphin's journey. Setting up the tonality and meter prior to this song will help the musical mind in sustaining Dorian tonality while dealing with the rhythmic complexity. Set up Unusual Paired meter with the beat grouping 2–3 (See Chapter 4). This song, expressively, demands the energy of movement through meter shifts, with the dance sections drawing the greatest intensity through pitch as well as rhythm, resolving to the calming end of the piece. Song architecture prompts expression so that children execute this song with the grace of the dolphin in and out of the water. Expression then enables vocal technique, as the melody undulates in descending and ascending line, using the energy of the line, meter, and momentum to power the voice through the peak of the dance. It draws even more energy in the repetition. Vocal placement and melodic contour of this song draw a lovely sound from children's voices. The ease and artistry with which children sing this song in all its complexity is as stunning as the dolphin.

Additional songs in this book that fit into this cluster of difficulty include *Penguin* (p. 42), *Autumn Thought* (p. 45), *Weasel* (p. 48), *Oh Star* (p. 51), *What Does Little Birdie Say?* (p. 23), *Night* (p. 86), and *Elephant* (p. 89). A group of children that competently sings your comprehensive set of five songs at this level is ready to rehearse them with piano accompaniments, creating a well-balanced concert program ready for performance. You can further broaden the number of tonalities or meters at this level by using as warm-ups any of the songs from the first cluster of songs, or the little art songs with translated haiku texts presented in Chapter 1, Etude 1, and Etude 2.

# Dolphin

**Figure 7.12**
Dorian, Multimetric—
Unusual Paired/Unusual
Unpaired/Triple

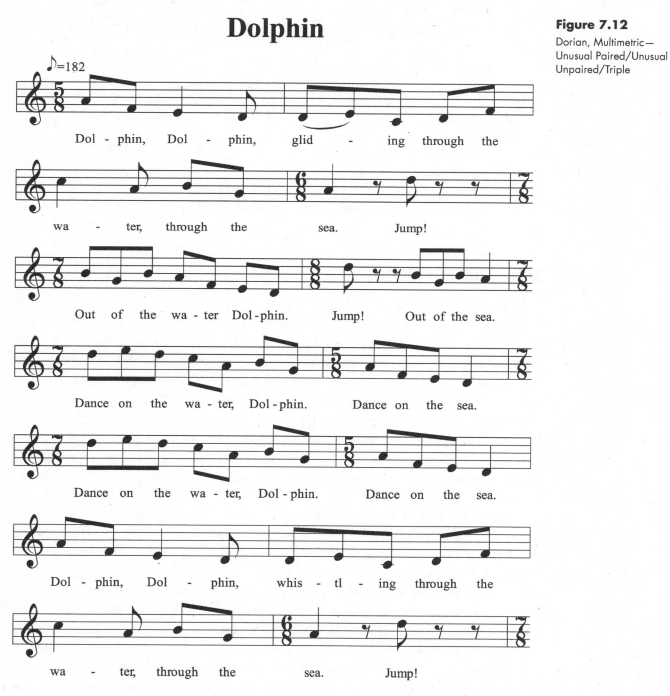

*continued on next page*

**Figure 7.12**
Continued

Out of the wa-ter Dol-phin. Jump! Out of the sea.

Dance on the wa-ter, Dol-phin. Dance on the sea.

Dance on the wa-ter, Dol-phin. Dance on the sea.

Dol-phin, Dol-phin, Dol-phin, Dol-phin,

Dol-phin, Dol-phin.

## Song Cluster 3

This cluster of songs is generally more difficult than the previous cluster, requiring greater musical and vocal maturity. Songs of this cluster, like those of the previous clusters, compel the musical mind, prompt artistic expression, and enable vocal technique, now at the more mature level of development. These songs serve children who have a background in tonalities and meters who have beautifully sung songs that give voice to children's artistry at the easier level. This cluster of songs serves a broad range of ages with some of the songs needing greater maturity than others. Songs of this cluster also work well as warm-ups with more developed singers. Use the Song Selection Guide that accompanies this Etude to help you in choosing a comprehensive set of songs at this level that includes a broad range of tonalities, meters, texts, expressions, and vocal challenges.

*April Rain Song* (Figure 7.13) engages children with the lovely words of Langston Hughes set in Aeolian tonality with meter shifting between Duple and Triple. Rests, ties, and upbeats increase the rhythm difficulty of this song beyond the subtle shifting of meters with common micro beats. Tonal supports the musical mind with its many stepwise passages and reinforcement of tonality. Melody and rhythm reflect the poetry and support each other as well as the text, prompting expression. The eloquence of Langston Hughes challenges children with the sophistication of text that addresses children's simple fascination with rain. The descriptive words address rain from the mundane to the sublime, making even gutters poetic. This song's greatest challenge is in expression, necessitating underlying momentum, gentle articulation of the staccato rain, yet

# April Rain Song

**Figure 7.13**

Aeolian, Multimetric—
Duple/Triple

111

sweeping melodic energy in the building of line. The vocal range serves children's voices, while the two 6/8 segments stretch vocal technique to power the voice with appropriate breath support for the energy of the line created by melodic contour and shift to Triple meter. Introducing this song with tonal and rhythm preps will format the musical mind to receive the tonality and meter. Rehearsing with movement will generate the momentum essential to this song, sustaining the common micro beats between meters, generating momentum, and making the energy of the line come alive with musical nuance. This song draws a lovely sound out of children with expression to match, inviting children to express their joy in the wonder of rain.

*Sea Anemone* (Figure 7.14), set in Phrygian tonality and Duple meter, creates a level of difficulty that belies its seeming simplicity. The rhythm of the word anemone becomes a motive throughout. It begins on an upbeat which increases rhythm difficulty and is followed each time with the challenge of long notes, jagged rhythms and ties. The

**Figure 7.14**
Phrygian, Duple

# Sea Anemone

relatively slow tempo increases difficulty, particularly through the long notes. The song demands more of the musical mind than one that more clearly defines both tonality and meter, increasing difficulty still more. Tonal contour helps to sustain Phrygian amidst the rhythm challenges, adding a bit of difficulty with the prominence of the fifth, which also concludes the song. The rhythmic motive with its consistent tonal pairing becomes a rather haunting figure, building tension with each repetition. The third repetition of the figure spins energy to the peak of the song with breath support and momentum. The growing intensity creates an expressive challenge with the energy of the line in contrast to the more subtle power of the repeated motive. Rhythm and tonal preps help to secure tonality and meter. Rehearsal with movement will assure the underlying meter through the long notes and generate momentum and energy of the line throughout. This song draws a lovely ensemble sound, calling attention to both the unusual beauty of the sea anemone and the unusual beauty of children's artistry.

# Fairies

**Figure 7.15**

Dorian, Multimetric—
Combined/Duple/Triple

113

*Fairies* (Figure 7.15), with the insightful words of Langston Hughes set in Dorian tonality with shifting meters, offers a challenge in expression that requires maturity of singers. The shifts between Combined, Duple, and Triple meters accommodate the expression of the words. Macro beats of equal duration throughout the meter changes are disrupted slightly by the single 9/8 measure in Triple meter which can feel more like three micro beats, each with Triple divisions. The necessary rubato throughout reflects the movement of the words, adding greater difficulty. Rhythm, tonal, and text support each other with rhythm and melody a musical translation of text. The vocal difficulty of this song is tied directly to the expressive difficulty, the greater challenge. The drama of building the energy of the line through melodic contour, rhythm, and elastic tempo propels tension to the peak of the song, before resolving in final reflection. Moving expression of this song empowers the voice with breath support and quality sound in the optimal range for children's voices. The song draws a lovely ensemble sound and genuine artistry from children. The musical nuance that comes alive in children moves the teacher as much as it does the children. Introducing this song with tonal and rhythm preps helps to secure tonality and meter in the musical mind, while rehearsal with movement will enhance all dimensions of execution. Set up Combined meter with the beat grouping 3–2 with equal macro beats to match the opening, even though the song moves quickly to duple meter. Children with the musical readiness for this song don't hesitate to sing about fairies, as they absorb the words and its musical expression with the reverence of poets and artists.

**Figure 7.16**
Lydian, Multimetric—
Unusual Paired/Unusual
Unpaired/Duple

# Snow Is Falling

**Snow is Falling** (Figure 7.16) presents considerable difficulty in Lydian tonality and shifting unusual meters, even with the immediate repetition of the first four measures and the later recurrence of the first eight measures. The ongoing snow falling in un-usual meters at a very quick tempo demands riveted attention, deliberate singing, and momentum. Melody, rhythm, and text support each other. The complex rhythm plus the fast tempo focuses the musical mind on rhythm rather than tonal, necessitating competence in Lydian tonality amidst rhythm challenges. The snow sets the stage for a child offering a gift of love in the middle section, with the near breathlessness that often accompanies it. Expressive challenges increase in the middle section, with singers having to sustain the quick pace and shifting meters while breaking somewhat melodically to offer the heartfelt gift, in contrast to the constancy of the falling snow. Vocal demands are in the realm of breath, slurs, and articulation. The fast-paced shifting meters with primarily one syllable words in the middle section create the necessity for clean articulation. The shift back into the insistent snow, without losing a beat, adds to the tension of the snow filled night. This song contrasts with the more lyric songs, encouraging children to bring the sound they have developed through those more lyric songs into the fast and furious *Snow is Falling*, expanding their artistry to quite a different type of musical experience. Using a tonality and meter prep will help to secure the difficult tonality and meter in the musical mind. Set the meter prep in Unusual Paired meter with the beat grouping 2–3, as that begins the song, even though the next measure is grouped 3–2 (See Chapter 4). Children at this level will easily navigate the changes in beat groupings as well as the shifting meters. Rehearsing with movement will make the driving meter more tangible while enhancing momentum and energy. The unselfish gift that children offer in this song is truly the beauty of their artistry.

## The Falling Star

**Figure 7.17**
Phrygian, Multimetric—
Triple/Duple

*The Falling Star* (Figure 7.17), with the lovely poem of Sara Teasdale set in Phrygian tonality and shifting Duple and Triple meters, offers quite an artistic experience for children at this level. Shifting meters with consistent micro beats offer rhythm challenge, as do upbeats, tie, and triplet, while tonal compels the musical mind and supports rhythm and text. This song begs for the flexibility of rubato, increasing difficulty, and the expression of this song is its greatest challenge. Rhythm and melody mirror the words, creating a drama that unfolds in singing and movement. The calm, initial statement is "blinded" by the energy of the text, expressed through sudden raised pitch and hastened rhythm. Searing urgency to get off the "burning" with accelerated tempo "too quick to hold" increases intensity in communicating the thrill of witnessing the falling star. The drama concludes with singers reflecting on what was experienced, a bit stunned by the fleeting moment, and hesitant to accept its impermanence. Singers become actors, directors, and producers of this little theater piece, enacting the drama of the words through their musical translation. The energy of expression enables necessary vocal technique, charging appropriate breath, supporting the leaps to the highest pitches, and bringing the sound and support in the upper register down to the full range of the song. Setting this song up with tonal and rhythm preps helps to secure tonality and meter. Rehearsal with movement serves to capture musical nuance, assuring momentum and creating the energy of the line. This song draws pure artistry out of children as they embody the expression of this song, complete with a lovely sound and the sensitivity of artists.

*The Bow that Bridges Heaven* (Figure 7.18) presents the lovely words of Christina Rossetti set in Mixolydian tonality shifting between Combined and Duple meter. This song offers quite a challenge to young artists both vocally and expressively. Rhythmic challenges include Combined meter, rest, ties, and upbeats, all of which reflect the rhythm of the words. Tonal, rhythm, and text support each other, with the sophistication of the text adding an element of difficulty. The expressive demands of this song, coupled with the vocal technique needed to deliver its potent expression, requires maturity in singers while fostering greater artistry. Christina Rossetti captures the ease yet agitation of the water, as if she wrote the opening in Combined meter, which then lends itself to the pondering of the clouds. Melodic contour reflects her words throughout, building the line phrase by phrase as she builds intensity to the stunning beauty of a rainbow, with a moment of awe before her final statement. The song itself prompts expression of the drama, as the energy of the line builds intensity to the peak of the song, inviting both singers and listeners to behold the wonder of the rainbow. Vocal placement draws a lovely sound from children, but the expression of this song enables greater vocal technique, as children engage appropriate breath support in order to deliver such moving expression. Introducing this song with tonal and rhythm preps will help to secure tonality and meter in the musical mind. Set up the Combined meter prep with the beat grouping 2–3 with macro beats of equal length, like the opening of the song. Children at this level will easily move between Combined and Duple meter, with Combined meter beat grouping either 2–3 or 3–2. Rehearsal with movement will secure meter and help children to build the energy of the line with the musical nuance inherent in this song. Children sing this song with the skill of young artists as they reflect the beauty of the rainbow, which in turn reflects the beauty of the children.

Additional songs presented in this book that fit into this cluster of difficulty include *Starfish* (p. 53), *African Dance* (p. 54), *May Night* (p. 55), and *The Bird's Carol* (p. 56). A group of children that competently sings your set of five songs at this level is ready to

# The Bow that Bridges Heaven

**Figure 7.18**
Mixolydian, Multimetric—
Combined/Duple
117

rehearse them with piano accompaniments, creating a well-balanced concert program. You can further broaden the number of tonalities or meters at this level by using as warm-ups any of the songs from the first or second cluster of songs, or the little art songs with translated haiku texts presented in Chapter 1, Etude 1, and Etude 2.

You have chosen for your children a set of songs that meets their musical needs rhythmically, tonally, expressively, and vocally that both challenges and supports their developing artistry. Your comprehensive set of songs includes a variety of tonalities, meters, texts, styles, expressions, and vocal challenges. Your set of songs can serve the music classroom, children's chorus, and concert program. Now broaden your song selection with additional songs that are worthy of children's artistry. Add to your chosen set that wonderful spiritual or folk song. Add that lovely song of the masters. Add that rousing song for its timely message or theatrical flair. The key is in sustaining an ongoing repertoire of unison songs of increasing musical difficulty that give voice to children's artistry throughout every level of development.

Let us lift our voices in song for the development of children's artistry. Let us review songs for children through the lens of giving voice to children's artistry. Let us select songs for our children that compel the musical mind, prompt artistic expression, and enable vocal technique—songs that inspire children's artistry.

# APPENDICES

## Meters

Rhythm examples in each meter present macro beats, micro beats, and divisions in relation to each other.

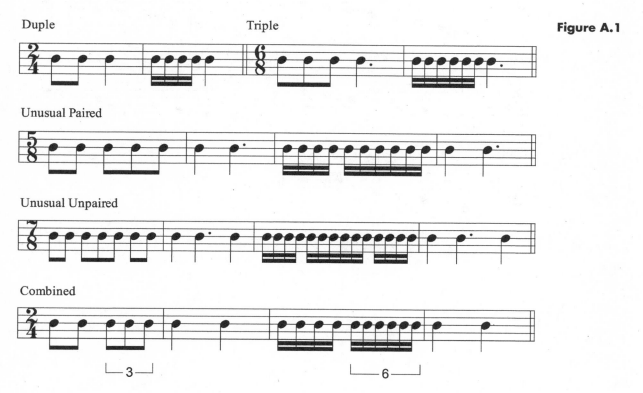

**Figure A.1**

*continued on next page*

## Tonalities

**Figure A.2**

# APPENDIX B  Weight Distribution with Various Beat Groupings in Unusual Meters Used in this Book

⇩Represents macro beat weight in the various beat groupings within each meter.

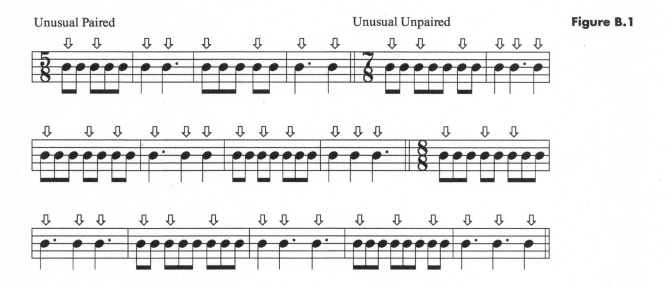

Unusual Paired          Unusual Unpaired          **Figure B.1**

# APPENDIX C  Characteristic Tones of Each Tonality

Characteristic tones of each tonality are presented here in relation to Major tonality. Each tonality on the left includes a major third, while those on the right each include a minor third.

↓ Characteristic tone one-half step lower than Major
↑ Characteristic tone one-half step higher than Major
☊ Characteristic tone of tonality, though same as Major, despite the minor third

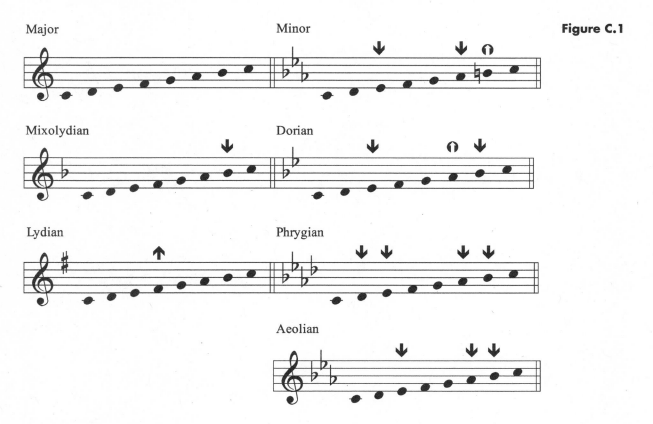

**Figure C.1**

## APPENDIX D  Harmonic Functions that Define Each Tonality

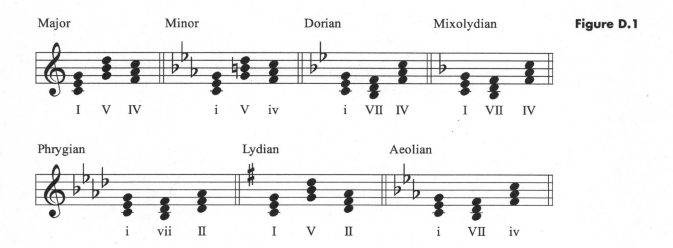

Figure D.1

# NOTES

## Chapter 1

1   Edwin Gordon always separated tonal from rhythm to teach tonal. Children of all ages and stages at the Come Children Sing Institute demonstrated through many years that children learn tonal better when it is presented with the simplest of rhythm. Early accounts of these findings are in Mary Ellen Pinzino, *Letters on Music Learning, Compiled Electronic Edition* (Homewood, IL: Self-published, 2007), 30–32.

2   Mary Ellen Pinzino, "Online Teacher Education Center: Tonal Difficulty," accessed August 6, 2021, self-published (subscription), https://www.comechildrensing.com/teachers/blog_details.php?type=local&blog_id=383&catCode=63.

3   For a detailed explanation of unusual meters, see Edwin E. Gordon, *Learning Sequences in Music: Skill, Content, and Patterns: A Music Learning Theory* 1997 ed. (Chicago: GIA Publications, Inc. 1997), 167–72.

## Chapter 2

1   Pinzino, *Letters*, 8–10.

2   Concepts gleaned from many years of discussion with Edwin Gordon, examined through decades in the classroom with all ages, have led to insights presented here. Many of Gordon's views can be found in Gordon, *Learning Sequences*.

3   Pinzino, *Letters*, 8–10.

4   Pinzino, *Letters*, 8–10.

5   Pinzino, "Online Teacher Education Center: The Bridge to Choral Singing," https://www.comechildrensing.com/teachers/blog_details.php?type=local&blog_id=379&catCode=64.

6   Mary Ellen Pinzino, "Awakening Artistry in the Choral Rehearsal," *International Choral Bulletin* XXV no. 2 (2nd Quarter, 2006): 8–9.

7   Pinzino, "Awakening Artistry," 12.

8   Pinzino, "Awakening Artistry," 12.

9   Pinzino, "Online Teacher Education Center: The Voice of Children's Artistry," https://www.comechildrensing.com/teachers/blog_details.php?type=local&blog_id=314&catCode=58.

10  Pinzino, "Online Teacher Education Center: The Voice of Children's Artistry," https://www.comechildrensing.com/teachers/blog_details.php?type=local&blog_id=314&catCode=58.

## Chapter 3

1   A full discussion of Gordon's views on rhythm can be found in Gordon, *Learning Sequences*, 161–201.

## Chapter 4

1   Edwin Gordon, "Sugarloaf Seminars on Music Learning," Annual, c. 1985–1993, Temple University Sugarloaf Conference Center, (now Chestnut Hill College, The Commonwealth Chateau at SugarLoaf).

2   Gordon, "Sugarloaf Seminars."

3   Gordon, "Sugarloaf Seminars."

4  Gordon, "Sugarloaf Seminars."

5  Pinzino, "Online Teacher Education Center: Vocal Range/Tempo/Neutral Syllables," https://www.comechildrensing.com/teachers/blog_details.php?type=local&blog_id=268&catCode=58.

## Etude 2

1  Gordon designed his rhythm syllables to be used only in the context of rhythm. They do serve well, however, with children who are familiar with the syllables in the context of rhythm, to draw attention to rhythm and meter in the context of song. Gordon's rhythm syllables can be found in Gordon, *Learning Sequences*, 78–83.

# BIBLIOGRAPHY

Gordon, Edwin E. *Learning Sequences in Music: Skill, Content, and Patterns: A Music Learning Theory.* 1997 ed., Chicago: GIA Publications, Inc., 1997.

Gordon, Edwin. "Sugarloaf Seminars on Music Learning." Temple University Sugarloaf Conference Center (now The Commonwealth Chateau at SugarLoaf), Annual, c. 1985–1993.

Pinzino, Mary Ellen. "Awakening Artistry in the Choral Rehearsal." *International Choral Bulletin* XXV, no. 2 (2nd Quarter, 2006), Chemin des Carreaux, France, International Federation for Choral Music.

Pinzino, Mary Ellen. *Letters on Music Learning, Compiled Electronic Edition.* Homewood, IL: Self-published, 2007.

Pinzino, Mary Ellen. "Online Teacher Education Center," accessed August 6, 2021, self-published (subscription). https://www.comechildrensing.com/teachers/.

Pinzino, Mary Ellen. "Song Library," accessed August 6, 2021, self-published (subscription). https://www.comechildrensing.com/song_library/.

# SONG INDEX

# INDEX